You Can Change Other People

Peter Bregman

Bestselling Author of *18 Minutes*

Howie Jacobson, PhD

You Can Change Other People

The Four Steps to Help Your Colleagues, Employees—Even Family—Up Their Game

WILEY

Published by John Wiley & Sons, Inc., Hoboken, New Jersey.
Published simultaneously in Canada.

For general information on our other products and services or for technical support, please contact our Customer Care Department within the United States at (800) 762-2974, outside the United States at (317) 572-3993 or fax (317) 572-4002.

Wiley publishes in a variety of print and electronic formats and by print-on-demand. Some material included with standard print versions of this book may not be included in e-books or in print-on-demand. If this book refers to media such as a CD or DVD that is not included in the version you purchased, you may download this material at http://booksupport.wiley.com. For more information about Wiley products, visit www.wiley.com.

Library of Congress Cataloging-in-Publication Data

Names: Bregman, Peter, author. | Jacobson, Howie, author.
Title: You can change other people : the four steps to help your
    colleagues, employees-even family-up their game / Peter Bregman, Howie
    Jacobson.
Description: First Edition. | Hoboken, New Jersey : Wiley, 2022.
Identifiers: LCCN 2021021827 (print) | LCCN 2021021828 (ebook) | ISBN
    9781119816539 (hardback) | ISBN 9781119816607 (adobe pdf) | ISBN
    9781119816591 (epub)
Subjects: LCSH: Communication in management. | Interpersonal relations. |
    Leadership.
Classification: LCC HD30.3 .B744 2022 (print) | LCC HD30.3 (ebook) | DDC
    650.1/3—dc23
LC record available at https://lccn.loc.gov/2021021827
LC ebook record available at https://lccn.loc.gov/2021021828

COVER DESIGN: PAUL MCCARTHY

SKY10028795_080521

We dedicate this book to the memory of our fathers:

Gerry Bregman   13 December 1931–23 April 2020

Joel R. Jacobson   30 July 1918–26 December 1989

Peter: Papa, every page in this book is inspired by the gentle, sweet way you always brought out the best in people.

Howie: Dad, you showed me how to be a warrior for positive change and a steadfast champion of the underdog.

CONTENTS

Foreword   xi

PART ONE:
A NEW WAY TO HELP PEOPLE
(BECAUSE THE OLD WAYS DON'T WORK)   1

Chapter 1
Why It's Important to Change Other People   3
Brian's $170,000,000 Turnaround

Chapter 2
People Don't Resist Change—They Resist
Being Changed   13
Yes, I Want That Third Bowl of Ice Cream!

Chapter 3
Power 1: Ownership   17
Whose Spreadsheet Is It Anyway?

Chapter 4
Power 2: Independent Capability   21
Spencer Thinks He's Helping, but He's Not

Chapter 5
Power 3: Emotional Courage   25
If You Are Willing to Feel Everything, You Can
Do Anything

Chapter 6
Power 4: Future-Proofing   29
Change Is a Future Thing

PART TWO: THE FOUR STEPS   **33**

STEP 1:
SHIFT FROM CRITIC TO ALLY   **35**
Chapter 7
Become an Ally   37
The Ramona Problem

Chapter 8
Be Your Own Ally First   41
Find Your Positive Intent

Chapter 9
Then Be Your Partner's Ally   47
Find Their Positive Intent

Chapter 10
How to Get Permission to Help   51
Silver Platter Opportunities

Chapter 11
How to Initiate the Conversation   59
Do You Have a Minute?

Chapter 12
Don't Rely on Your Position of Power   71
Are You Willing to Try Something?

Chapter 13
Stay on Track 75
Pitfalls to Avoid

STEP 2:
IDENTIFY AN ENERGIZING OUTCOME 81

Chapter 14
Problems Are Signposts Pointing to Energizing
Outcomes 83
No More Code, No More Bugs

Chapter 15
Make It Positive 91
Transform "Don't Want" into "Do Want"

Chapter 16
Make It Clear 95
Get to Shared Clarity

Chapter 17
Make It Meaningful 99
Get to What Matters

STEP 3:
FIND THE HIDDEN OPPORTUNITY 103

Chapter 18
Become a Scientist 105
They're Not Learning from You; They're Learning with You

Chapter 19
Question 1: What's Happening Now? 115
Explore the Problem in Depth

Chapter 20
Question 2: What Have You Tried?   125
What Worked and What Didn't?

Chapter 21
Question 3: How Can You Use the Problem
to Achieve Your Energizing Outcome?   133
Thank Goodness for This Problem

Chapter 22
How Not to Get Distracted   157
Keep Your GPS On

STEP 4:
CREATE A LEVEL-10 PLAN   **163**

Chapter 23
Craft the Plan   165
Move from Insight to Traction

Chapter 24
Task 1: Identify Options   167
Let's Put That on the List. What Else Might You Try?

Chapter 25
Task 2: Choose the Path Forward   185
If You Did Know, What Would It Be?

Chapter 26
Task 3: Commit to the Plan   197
What, How, and When?

Chapter 27
Taking the Four Steps into Your World   209
You Can Change Other People

Acknowledgments   **213**

About the Authors   **219**

FOREWORD

As one of the founders of the field of business coaching and an executive coach for more than 40 years, my mission has been simple: to help great leaders get even better through positive, lasting behavioral change. It's been an incredibly rewarding career. I've coached CEOs at organizations like Ford, the World Bank, Best Buy, Target, the Girl Scouts, and many others. I get paid very well; I work with amazing people; I contribute to positive change in the world.

But perhaps my biggest thrill is when I help someone "against the odds"—someone whose colleagues and family members may have given up hope that they will ever change—because, while the mission is easy to understand, the practice of changing is infinitely harder.

Think about all the ways you've attempted to enact change in your own life: losing weight, spending more time with family, listening better, exercising more often, drinking more water, staying focused on long-term goals. How many of these goals have become permanent?

From my research with leaders, clients, and colleagues, the typical answer is "None." There is a period of high motivation and through sheer force of will, you'll remain conscientious on drinking your water, mustering the energy to go to the gym all week, or making an effort to listen intently during conversations.

Then life takes over. You get busy, unexpected events happen, and you justify all the reasons you can't remain focused on your goals this week. Months later, your gym attendance is inconsistent at best, and no one thinks you've improved your listening.

Worse yet than having failed at making these changes for your own life, how often have you tried to change the behavior of a parent, child, friend, partner, spouse, colleague, or employee? How did that go for you?

The sentence beginning "If only you just . . ." does not normally lead to a productive conversation around positive changes and strategies to help the person you care about do things differently. In fact, more often than not, it results in the person becoming instantly defensive, angry, and resentful!

And yet with my coaching tools and skills and mindsets at the ready, miracles do happen! My clients shift longstanding patterns of self-sabotage. They adopt and maintain positive new behaviors that help them achieve their ambitions and aspirations.

Words cannot describe how meaningful, how satisfying, and how joyful this work is. You just have to experience it for yourself.

What I can put in words, however, is how absolutely *possible* it is. Yes, you CAN change other people. I do it all the time. So do Peter and Howie.

And the book you're holding in your hands right now will give you everything you need to master the process.

Because it is a process. It's methodical, not magical or manipulative. It doesn't take any particular personality trait other than a sincere desire to help and the humility and discipline to learn something new and practice it diligently.

In fact, the principles in this book underpin what I and other top coaches do to help our successful clients get even better. What Peter and Howie have done in these pages makes what we do accessible to you, to use at work, at home, and anywhere you want to help those you care about achieve their potential. They've taken what most people consider to be a frustrating, ambiguous process and formulated the four key steps to change—for both yourself and others.

Working with Peter for many years, it's been our business to change other people's behaviors in ways that get noticed by the people around them. I have been ranked as the #1 executive coach in the world for many years, and Peter is my successor to that title. His expert knowledge is evident from the way he's laid out the methodology for leading people to change without throwing up those usual blocks of frustration and resentment. These steps guide you to be the kind of leader who encourages and builds their team to get the best results from them, empowering these individuals to grow and improve.

Read on and learn how to become a better leader, partner, parent, and friend today. You can start having the same impact on your world as the most sought-after coaches have in theirs.

Life is good.

—Marshall Goldsmith
New York Times #1 Bestselling Author of *Triggers*, *Mojo*, and *What Got You Here Won't Get You There*

YOU CAN CHANGE OTHER PEOPLE

PART ONE

A NEW WAY TO HELP PEOPLE (BECAUSE THE OLD WAYS DON'T WORK)

CHAPTER 1

WHY IT'S IMPORTANT TO CHANGE OTHER PEOPLE

BRIAN'S $170,000,000 TURNAROUND

When my client Brian Gaffney stepped into the role of CEO of Allianz Global Distributors, a financial services company with over $90 billion in assets, the company was losing $30 million a year. Not only was Allianz struggling, but the entire industry was in turmoil (many other asset management companies were closing their doors) and morale was low.

"My team is made up of incredibly talented people," Brian told me a short while after assuming the role. "But most of them have issues that are getting in the way of their effectiveness. One is rubbing people the wrong way by clumsy communications. Another isn't being clear with direct reports and isn't managing people effectively. A third needs to be more proactive; he isn't having hard conversations that need to happen. A fourth is brilliant but sloppy, and several people are commenting on the risk to his credibility."

So we went to work. And under Brian's leadership, a declining company made a complete turnaround. In the period that we worked together, he turned that $30 million loss into an annual profit of $140 million.

3

Here's what's really important about this story: Brian's turnaround at Allianz happened with the same leadership team that had been losing $30 million a year.

In other words, in a few short years, under Brian's leadership, the same people who were struggling with all those issues—the people who were leading the company to a damaging, unsustainable loss—*changed*.

And it was Brian who helped them change. By doing and saying specific things. Things that moved strong-willed individuals in positive, productive ways. Things that had a business-saving impact on revenue and profitability.

What Brian did was not magic. Neither was it the product of Brian's charisma or powers of persuasion. It was straightforward, methodical, and replicable. And you can do it too, in your world.

What you need is a process.

CAN YOU REALLY CHANGE OTHER PEOPLE?

You can't change other people; you can only change yourself. It's a truism.

Only it's not true.

I[1] know this—with 100 percent certainty—because it's my job to change other people. As an executive coach for CEOs and senior leaders in organizations of all sizes, my success depends on it.

Helping others change and improve when it's hard and when they may not want to (at first) can look and feel like magic, but it's not. It's a skill—a set of repeatable steps—that I've studied, developed, and honed over 30 years of practice.

---

[1]Throughout the book, "I" refers to Peter.

And it's teachable because I've taught it to people who have become some of the best coaches in the world.

By the time you finish this book, you'll have that skill too, which is important, because we all *need* the skill. No matter your role at work and in life, your success is dependent, at least in part, on the success of those around you. In many situations, it would be great for *you* if people changed for the better.

Just about all of the time, though, it would be better for *them* too: an employee who's more capable than they realize, who could be taking on bigger projects. A bright colleague who, if only they spoke up and shared their perspective, could have a positive impact on the team and, consequently, their success in the company. A boss whose visionary strategy would finally get traction if they focused more, resisting the distraction of bright, shiny objects.

For many of us, helping people change is not just a nice-to-have skill; it's a requirement. If you're a leader or manager in an organization, it's your job to change others: to transform squabbling coworkers into a capable team. To turn excuse-makers into responsibility-takers. To help high-potential contributors overcome dysfunctional habits and achieve their potential.

Changing others is perhaps the most important capability a leader can develop.

And yet it's a capability that most people lack. We avoid difficult conversations or handle them in ways that make things worse. We generate resistance rather than change. We point out how we want people to improve, but we lack the skills to get them there. We try to help and end up doing their work for them, making them dependent on us, when we should be helping them grow their independent capability. When emotions run high, we can even damage those relationships.

We feel stuck between a rock and a hard place: caring too much to keep our mouths shut, yet regretting the ineffective and hurtful things we say.

If only there were a third option.

There is. In this book, I will show you exactly why what you've been doing hasn't been working, and I will teach you what to do instead.

I'll share my process, which I call the **Four Steps**. I have yet to find a more elegant, kind, and effective method for helping people make the changes they want and need to make in their work and their lives.

Rather than inviting resistance, the Four Steps generate ownership. Rather than fostering dependence, they create independent capability. Rather than strain the relationship between you and the person you're helping, the Four Steps grow and deepen your relationships.

The ability to help other people change, even when they've been stuck for years, and even when they don't believe they can, is a superpower. Up until now, this superpower has been an esoteric skill set, honed and used by some of the world's most effective coaches. In this book, I'm going to deconstruct that superpower so you can practice and master it.

Using the Four Steps, I helped one CEO of a high-tech company grow revenue from $350 million to over a billion as its stock price soared from $19 to $107. At another company, the senior team began working together, helping rather than criticizing each other, and their stock price tripled in a year. When leaders skillfully help each other—and the people around them—up their game, exceptional results follow.

When I teach the Four Steps to CEOs and their leadership teams, the positive results cascade throughout the organization, generating independently capable teams that perform at much higher levels than before. People work together better and accept more accountability. People own their mistakes and failures, set and achieve higher goals, and resist the temptation of behaviors that get in the way.

Over years of doing this work, I discovered something wonderful: The C-suite leaders I work with reported that not only are they more effective at their jobs, and not only are their employees stepping up and becoming leaders in their own right, but their personal lives are easier and more satisfying as well. They stopped fighting with, and micromanaging, their kids. They had more empowering conversations with their spouses. And they found themselves helping others dig out of ruts that were sometimes decades in the making.

My coauthor, Howie, in addition to his work with business clients, also uses the Four Steps to help people change destructive lifelong habits and regain their health. While doctors acknowledge that lifestyle can be as powerful as drugs and surgery, most don't offer this option to patients in the belief that they won't comply. Yet Howie's clients change their lifestyles all the time. One became a competitive triathlete, losing sixty pounds in the process. Another reversed his type 2 diabetes and reduced his blood pressure meds by 75 percent through dietary changes, daily exercise, and meditation practice. A third finally got off the binge/diet/binge cycle, for the first time in her life maintaining a healthy weight free "from the impending doom of relapse."

Let's banish the pain that comes from trying to change others in frustrated, angry ways—complaining, attacking, and manipulating them to get them to act differently. Those tactics cause tremendous damage. They don't feel good to anyone involved. And they *don't* work.

The Four Steps *do* work. And they heal relationships as people become allies instead of enemies, choosing skillful support over clumsy, destructive criticism.

Once you begin using the Four Steps, your world will feel lighter. You'll be happier. The people around you will be happier. You'll all get more done.

I wrote this book because that's the world I want to live in. A world where we build ownership, capability, and courage all around us. Where, rather than lashing out as annoyed critics, we reach out as allies. A world where we help raise people up to be the best they can be. And where they make us better people in return.

I'm grateful that you're taking the time to read this book. Thank you.

A TOUR OF THE BOOK

Before you start using the Four Steps, it's important to understand why they work, which I'll cover in Part One.

PART ONE: A NEW WAY TO HELP PEOPLE (BECAUSE THE OLD WAYS DON'T WORK)

First, I'll debunk the myth that people resist change and explain why so many of our efforts to change others fail **(Chapter 2)**.

Then I'll introduce you to the four powers that a person needs in order to change: ownership, independent capability, emotional courage, and future-proofing **(Chapters 3–6)**.

If someone doesn't change, they are missing at least one of these powers.

And when you use the Four Steps to help someone change, what you're really doing is igniting these powers in them so they change themselves. In Part Two, I'll teach you to do just that.

PART TWO: THE FOUR STEPS

This is the practical "how-to" portion of the book. To illustrate the Four Steps, we'll follow one scenario all the way from the initial problem to a detailed plan of action. You'll listen in on the conversation at the beginning of each step. Then we'll debrief that step in the following chapters, exploring underlying principles, dos and don'ts, and exceptions.

Here's a brief description of each step:

Step 1: Shift from Critic to Ally (Chapters 7–13) This is the magic move. It gets you to the place where your conversation partner[2] agrees to receive your help. You'll learn how to initiate conversations that help others change. Even better, you'll learn to recognize and capitalize on "silver platter" opportunities, times when people come to you already open to you helping them change—everyday opportunities that are easy to spot once you know what to look for. Start with this step and you'll move quickly past any potential resistance, well positioned as a trusted guide to help your partner change.

Step 2: Identify an Energizing Outcome (Chapters 14–17) This step shifts your partner from focusing on the problem to focusing on the outcome they want. It's a deceptively simple reorientation that moves people from frustration to excitement. For many years I didn't think this was such a big deal, but my clients tell me focusing on the desired outcome is not an obvious thing to do when they're mired in a difficult situation. It reliably gives them the right focus, exposing new and creative ways forward.

---

[2]Throughout this book, I refer to the person you want to help as your *partner* with plural pronouns (*their*, *them*, etc.). I hope this helps you orient yourself toward them in a supportive, friendly, and collaborative way.

Step 3: Find the Hidden Opportunity (Chapters 18–22)
In this step you return to the problem, but now you use it as
an opportunity to achieve the outcome in a creative or unexpected way. Here's where you can help people change so that
they not only get out of the mess they're in, but emerge at a
whole new level of functioning.

Step 4: Create a Level-10 Plan (Chapters 23–27) In this
final step you help your partner generate, refine, and commit
to a specific action plan to achieve their energizing outcome.
You're going for a "Level-10" plan, where they know exactly
what they're going to do and are confident they can do it. This
final step turns insight into action and intentions into impact.

Those are the Four Steps: Ally, Outcome, Opportunity,
Plan. If you're into mnemonics, think of "Ally-OOP," which,
appropriately, sounds like the basketball pass that sets your
teammate up for a slam dunk.

The companion website to this book (BregmanPartners.
com/change) shares sample "partner dialogues" that demonstrate the Four Steps in different contexts. You'll find typical Four-Step conversations around hard issues that vary by
domain (work and personal), power dynamic (supervisor/
employee, spouses, parent/child, friends), and topic (work
performance, health, relationship, personal goals). Before you
have your first Four-Step conversation with a partner, read
the sample dialogue that is most similar to the situation. It
will help you find the right words to say and what kinds of
responses you might expect from your partner.

★★★

Although I share important principles about personal
change, especially in the first few chapters, this is not a con-
ceptual book. *You Can Change Other People* is a user's manual,
meant to be as practical as possible.

Don't wait until you've mastered the Four Steps to start using them to help people change. Transparency is part of this process. You should feel free to share exactly what you're doing and why you're doing it. Tell the truth: "Hey, I got this book and I think I can use the process to help you. I'm new at this, so it may not look smooth and polished. In fact, I might even pause and refer to the text from time to time. Are you open to that?"

Once you've read the book and practiced a few times, you will quickly grow your capability and confidence to use the Four Steps to help the people around you live fuller, richer, more powerful, and more authentic lives.

First, though, let's dispel the myth that people resist change.

CHAPTER 2

PEOPLE DON'T RESIST CHANGE— THEY RESIST *BEING* CHANGED

YES, I WANT THAT THIRD BOWL OF ICE CREAM!

Let me say up front, with a father's pride, that my 13-year-old son Daniel is one of the smartest, most talented people I know. He's quick, charming, and witty—and he's the poster child for resistance. Even a basic direction—"Go brush your teeth"—elicits tremendous pushback.

But when Daniel sets his mind to something, his drive, enthusiasm, and persistence are unstoppable. He will change and raise his game in all sorts of ways. Case in point: a gaming PC. He wanted it, but I wouldn't buy it for him. So he went to work, formulating a plan to make enough money to afford it on his own.

He asked his grandfather for an inexpensive drone for his birthday. He spent hours mastering it, learning how to shoot aerial video footage and eventually impressing his Aunt Catherine enough that she hired him to go with her to South Carolina for a week and shoot footage for her real estate company. He was nervous about making the trip by himself but decided to do it. He packed his own bag—no nagging required. He made a stellar video . . . and $650.

The computer he wanted was still way out of his budget. Undeterred, he discovered a way: He would buy the parts and build it himself. He educated himself on cases, motherboards, graphics cards, fans, and the rest, and ordered them from various websites. He enlisted his cousin Atticus to help him build it. After three months of overcoming obstacles, he finally had his gaming PC.

In order to get what he wanted, Daniel had to change. He learned new skills, started a business, found a client, overcame fears, asked for help, and solved challenging problems— all this from the kid who wouldn't brush his teeth when I asked him to.

Daniel wasn't resistant to change. He was resistant to *being* changed.

People change all the time on their own. They make big changes like starting businesses, getting married, moving, or getting a new job. And they make smaller changes, like eating healthier, waking up earlier, or listening better.

But people change when *they choose* to change. If they feel like you're trying to *make* them change? Forget it.

The problem isn't a lack of skills, tactics, or strategy. Most of the time, people *know* exactly what to do. They're just not doing it. And it's that gap between what they know and what they do that's the challenge. Telling someone who's overeating sugar to "stop eating sugar" is profoundly unhelpful.

When people struggle with a problem, they often feel shame at their own inadequacy. The very fact that they want or need your help means, to them, that they've already failed. They think some version of "I should be able to handle this on my own. What's wrong with me?"

Now, imagine that you understand their problem and have a great idea that can help them. If you share your solution right away, and they haven't thought of it themselves, that will often bring their shame to the surface. And shame is inhibitory; that is, when people feel shame, they stop taking action. Unlike guilt, which says, *I did a bad thing,* and can motivate people to change, shame says, *I am a bad person*, and typically represses initiative and halts momentum.

Here's why: Shame is one of the feelings human beings will do almost anything not to feel. And the easiest way to get rid of shame—at least temporarily—is denial. If you deny the source of the shame, you deny that you have a problem (or deny that it's *your* problem). Presto: no shame.

But, of course, denying the problem, or the severity of the problem, or the consequences of the problem, means denying the need to change, which we then call *resistance to change*.

Unfortunately, most of what we try to do to help people change reinforces their shame. When we barge in with the answer or think we can do it better, or when we think they should know better, we reinforce their shame. That's why simply telling people what to do, or what we did in a similar situation, or what we *would* do if we were in that situation, so often backfires.

We give advice; they hear criticism.

I know I do. When I reach for the pint of Ben and Jerry's to fill up my third bowl of ice cream and anyone—my wife, my children, a concerned friend—asks, "Do you really want that third bowl of ice cream?" no matter how stuffed I am, I can assure you that I will answer with a loud "YES" and then add some extra fudge on top in defiance.

Here's what's crazy: I really do want to stop eating sugar. And I also know that they want to be helpful. They don't mean to criticize me. (Technically, they're just asking me a question.) I know they love and care for me. But I am also ashamed to admit, at that moment, that I'm out of control. It feels weak to say, "You're right. I can't control myself."

So I don't. I double-down on my mistake in order to say, "I'm in control!"

I know you don't mean to be a critic when you give advice. But if the people you're trying to help feel that you're coming at them with an air of "I know better than you" or "The answer is simple; just do X," they'll dig in their heels and resist change.

But that doesn't mean there isn't a way to help them change. We just have to let go of unsolicited advice and explanations.

As I write this, Daniel is gaming on the new computer that he changed his life to build. People can overcome great odds to follow through on what they want. But we won't help them get there by criticizing what they're doing, telling them what to do, or trying to motivate them to do something different.

Fortunately, there are ways we *can* help.

We can develop a person's ownership, independent capability, emotional courage, and future-proofing, so they change themselves. In the next four chapters, we'll explore each of those powers, starting with ownership.

CHAPTER 3

POWER 1: OWNERSHIP

WHOSE SPREADSHEET IS IT ANYWAY?

Spencer,[1] the CEO of a technology company, was worried. The company's customer growth rate was too low.

So Spencer did some digging and realized that Marketing wasn't producing enough leads. History showed that a certain number of leads would predictably convert into customers. That conversion rate was steady, but the leads had dropped off.

The solution was straightforward: more leads, more customers.

So Spencer started nudging, cajoling, and probing to get better data from Marketing about leads. Weeks later, he still hadn't gotten a straight answer. In exasperation, he asked his Chief Marketing Officer, Octavia, to create a weekly marketing report and have it in his inbox by 10 a.m. each Monday.

When Spencer looked at the first report, his eyes glazed over. He was staring at a complex spreadsheet, complete with pivot tables, a dozen different background colors, and so

---

[1]A note about the fictional names for the composite characters in this book: I've tried to be inclusive and avoid gender, cultural, and racial stereotyping. If any of the names or pronouns rub you the wrong way, feel free to change them.

much data that the key numbers were obscured by hundreds of unimportant ones.

In frustration, Spencer took 30 minutes and simplified the report to show just two columns: goal and performance against the goal. He then emailed it to Octavia, telling her that her report didn't distinguish signal from noise and that she should use his new one from now on.

He figured she'd be happy because the new report took far less time to complete and offered a much clearer picture of how things stand.

Is that how Octavia felt when she received his email?

Sadly and predictably, no. Octavia felt unappreciated, misunderstood, and angry. First, she'd spent the entire weekend working on the spreadsheet, collating numbers from multiple sources and getting more and more annoyed at the company's fragmented approach to customer relationship management (CRM).

Second, Spencer totally misunderstood what Octavia wanted him to see. To her, the topline numbers were meaningless without context. What was the value in simply knowing that their lead flow last week missed the target by 45 percent? The important data were in the details: registration and conversion rates of the marketing webinars, the number of participants who watched long enough to hear the call to action, and important things like that. In her view, the details were critical.

And third, how was Octavia supposed to guess exactly what Spencer wanted when he hadn't even articulated what he needed the spreadsheet for in the first place?

What Spencer did, in his effort to get the result he wanted *and* to be helpful, was take ownership of the report away from Octavia. Now every time she filled it out, she was mindlessly complying with his demands. Even if Spencer's way was better, and took a tenth of the time to complete, she was still resentful. She wasn't proud of the report. It had no imprint of her thinking or caring on it. She didn't own it.

Consider two scenarios:

A. You come up with an idea you want to try.
B. Someone else comes up with an idea that they want you to try.

Which scenario do you think would be more motivating to you? Which scenario do you think would drive you to work harder to make it successful?

Almost everyone says Scenario A. Why? Pride of ownership is motivating.

Behavioral economist Dan Ariely found that test subjects who created their own origami cranes valued them five times higher than did outside observers. And when the instructions were made purposely unclear, leading to greater effort and uglier cranes, the creators valued them even more dearly.

When we own something, we care about it, so we'll take initiative on it and persist through thick and thin to see it through. We don't have to be supervised, held accountable, or rewarded or punished. Doing a good job, being proactive, being accountable for outcomes, and dealing with problems are just part of our identity.

Scenario B, on the other hand, sabotages that ownership.

Because it's not our idea, it's *theirs*. And when someone tries to impose their solution or advice on us, we tend to resist or, at best, execute it half-heartedly. If the action fails, we're more likely to blame their bad idea, versus our own inability to execute.

After all, an outsider's idea will often neglect the nuance of the situation, miss critical elements that we understand more intimately, and ignore personality issues that should inform a solution.

So what could Spencer have done differently?

He could have guided Octavia to think about how she could redo the report herself in a way that focused on the most important customer growth rate metrics. He could have modeled accountability by acknowledging that he hadn't clearly communicated the purpose of the report. And he could have brainstormed with Octavia on how it would be used, and by whom, and to make what decisions.

She would have gained some independent capability *and* felt pride of ownership over the simplified report, knowing it was having a company-wide impact. Getting her to complete it on time every week wouldn't have been a struggle or source of simmering resentment. Rather, Octavia would likely have wanted to broadcast the report throughout the organization, both to share helpful and timely information, and to build her career capital and influence. As the architect and owner of the report, Octavia would have become a more energetic and proactive force for good in the company.

Remember my son Daniel who bought and built his own gaming computer? He owned the entire process. He wanted the computer; I didn't want it for him. He enlisted help—from his grandfather, aunt, cousin, and even me at times—to take the necessary steps in the process. He didn't take shortcuts. He put up with frustration, confusion, and fear without giving up.

That's what ownership looks like.

When you solve problems for others, you take away their ownership of those solutions. Even if your advice is perfect—which, by the way, is almost never the case—it's useless if it won't be used.

If you really want to change someone, get them to create the plan. Get them to defend it. They'll be much more likely to implement a suboptimal plan of *their* creation and choosing than the perfect plan that you create. And if their initial plan fails? You'll be in a position to help them brainstorm a different approach because they'll see you as an ally, rather than a critic.

Personal ownership is one important power of change. Another, as we're about to see, is independent capability.

CHAPTER 4

POWER 2: INDEPENDENT CAPABILITY

SPENCER THINKS HE'S HELPING, BUT HE'S NOT

So, Spencer rejected Octavia's report and replaced it with his own design, which she had to update each week, momentarily solving his problem but robbing her of ownership and creating a tense relationship between them.

Let's consider a completely different way this could have played out.

Suppose Spencer had directed Octavia to create the report, but instead of spending her weekend putting together the wrong thing, Octavia had simply asked him what it should look like.

In that case, would it have been fine for Spencer to design the spreadsheet for her? That way, Octavia would not have wasted her weekend, Spencer would not have had to critique her poorly conceived, overly detailed report, and Octavia would not be left feeling resentful.

This scenario would be tempting for both of them. Octavia, of course, might be happy and relieved because she gets a quick answer and now can fill out the spreadsheet (or have someone else fill it out mindlessly) in full confidence that she's providing exactly the right information. And Spencer would be happy too: He gets the crucial data he wants in the brief format he prefers. He also gets to feel helpful and smart, qualities that won him the CEO post in the first place. And he receives positive feedback from Octavia, who is both impressed with his competence and grateful for his assistance. It's a win-win!

Or is it?

While Octavia is now compiling a report that meets Spencer's expectations, she hasn't changed. She's no more strategic or proactive than before. She's no more discerning about the problem and potential solutions. And when you think about the underlying problem—an underperforming Marketing Department—what's going to make a bigger difference: Octavia's ability to input numbers into spreadsheet cells or her ability to think strategically and act proactively in the marketplace? Spencer missed a crucial opportunity to raise the performance of a department.

A person undergoing real, lasting change must become independently capable so they aren't in constant need of someone else in order to follow through.

At one level, that's so obvious, I might not need to mention it. If I can't create a spreadsheet, then I won't be able to create a spreadsheet. But we're not just talking about a spreadsheet here. Spreadsheets don't solve problems; people do. We're talking about *thinking strategically* in order to solve a problem.

I'd argue that the real opportunity for change here is for Octavia to understand the revenue problem they're facing, understand how Marketing's poor lead generation is contributing to it, and most important, own it and be able to turn it around.

In other words, Spencer's real prize here isn't a great spreadsheet, it's a marketing leader who is able to bring about sustainable growth in sales and profits.

By relying on Spencer to create the spreadsheet, Octavia doesn't have to grow. She doesn't have to become more strategic, or more thoughtful, or a better problem solver. She doesn't even need to become a better marketer.

Which means that every time the business needs support from Marketing, someone—probably Spencer—will have to shoulder the burden that Octavia is unable to carry. Octavia remains an order taker, not a thoughtful, insightful problem-solving partner.

Being helpful can be a wonderful trait in a manager or colleague—even a family member. And there are times when it's appropriate (if I can't figure out how to unmute myself in a Zoom meeting, and you tell me to click on the microphone icon in the lower left of my screen, that's great).

But if someone comes to you with a recurring problem or one that requires their thinking and judgment, then giving them the answer or doing it for them will function as a crutch. You will have missed an opportunity to build their independent capability. And the next time they have a similar problem, they'll just come to you again, because they haven't learned how to solve it. They haven't changed. You will be stuck doing their work and they will be stuck at a lower level of performance.

That's the outcome Spencer got when he spent 30 minutes creating the new spreadsheet. What he should have done instead is grow Octavia's capacity to act more powerfully and successfully in the future.

Ownership and capability are essential to making that happen. But there's more. Even if someone you're helping has ownership and capability, change is emotionally difficult. Your partner will need the power of emotional courage to learn unfamiliar and uncomfortable new behaviors. We'll explore this in the next chapter.

CHAPTER 5

POWER 3: EMOTIONAL COURAGE

IF YOU ARE WILLING TO FEEL EVERYTHING, YOU CAN DO ANYTHING

What if, instead of criticizing her spreadsheet or redoing it, Spencer sat down with Octavia to help her grow her ownership of the problem and increase her capability to solve it?

Are they done?

Not so fast. There's something missing. A challenge that is rarely addressed yet causes many failed change attempts: the massive gap between knowing what to do and actually doing it.

Change is hard. And admitting that you need to change can be very hard. Facing colleagues and asking for their help in changing can be extremely hard. And struggling to develop new skills can be downright terrifying, especially when you have to give up old familiar patterns without yet having developed new ones to replace them.

Octavia needs the courage to feel all those uncomfortable feelings, even as she acts in ways that trigger and intensify them.

Think for a moment about a conversation you know you should have with someone, yet haven't. Is there an issue you're reluctant to share with a partner? A conflict at work that you're not addressing? Subpar performance from someone you're responsible for?

Why haven't you had that conversation yet?

Is it because you're not motivated? Because you just don't care enough to bother? I doubt it. The very fact that it's on your mind indicates that you can feel its importance.

Is it because you don't have the knowledge or skills to have the conversation? You don't know what to say? How to say it? I'd bet you know exactly what you want to say and I'm sure you're skilled enough to say it. In fact, I imagine you've been thinking about it over the course of some time. Sure, you could tweak the words, maybe make them more elegant, but you know what you need to convey.

Is it because you don't have the time? Haven't had the opportunity? Again, in my experience, that's not really standing in your way. When something's important, you make the time. You find the opportunity or proactively create it.

Those are usually the things that we try to solve for when we want to make change: *motivation, knowledge, skills, time,* and *opportunity.* And they are the things that companies try to solve for—with communication plans, training programs, and time management—when attempting to spread change throughout their organizations. But those are not the things that, in the end, prevent people from moving forward.

So then what's stopping you?

Feeling.

Think about it. If you have that conversation, you'll likely feel something uncomfortable. Something you're avoiding. Something you don't want to feel.

Maybe your partner will respond badly, and you'll get into an argument. Maybe they'll feel hurt, and you'll feel bad for having hurt them. Maybe they'll get defensive and accuse you of a bunch of things, triggering your shame, and you'll respond defensively. Maybe they'll just get quiet and stone-faced and shut down communication entirely. Maybe you'll lose your temper.

But if you don't have the conversation, you won't have to feel what you don't want to feel. It's a simple and reliable strategy: If you don't want to feel uncomfortable, don't do things that feel uncomfortable.

Although this approach may be simple and reliable, it's not useful. It leads to procrastination and dysfunction. What can you do instead? Expand your capacity to feel uncomfortable feelings. Build your emotional courage—and theirs.

If they are willing to feel everything, they can do anything.

Stoking your partner's emotional courage will enable them to follow through on actions that feel uncomfortable, or even downright scary.

When Daniel decided to go, by himself, to South Carolina to shoot drone video footage with his Aunt Catherine, that was a big moment of independence. He had never taken a weeklong trip like that before. It was scary. And during shooting one day, when the wind picked up, he decided that it wasn't safe to send the drone up. People pressured him to risk it since they didn't want to lose a day of shooting, but he held firm. He could not have done all of that without emotional courage.

In the case of Octavia, when she is willing to feel vulnerable and less than competent as she struggles to master a new skill set, she will risk putting herself in the necessary conversations and situations that she must have if she is to change.

What Spencer can do here is to encourage Octavia to work on that spreadsheet, even - in fact, especially - if it means she'll have to spend time in her "discomfort zone."

As you can probably tell by now, when I say you can change other people, I'm going for a higher bar than simply getting them to deliver you a spreadsheet. I'm talking about fundamental and sustainable change. Helping someone develop ownership, independent capability, and emotional courage is essential.

And there's one more important piece. As we'll see in the next chapter, for someone to change in a sustainable way, they need to be future-proof.

CHAPTER 6

POWER 4: FUTURE-PROOFING

CHANGE IS A FUTURE THING

Let's do a quick recap: People change when they take ownership, develop independent capability, and exercise emotional courage in the face of fears and setbacks. Our success changing others requires developing these traits in the people we're helping.

But we don't just want people to change for *this* moment. We want them to transform their sticky problems and unfulfilled desires into an opportunity to get better, stronger, and more resilient in the future. To bounce back from that next challenge and grow to meet future opportunities. That's future-proofing.

One of the downsides of giving advice or solving someone else's problem is that they lose out on the future benefits of their current struggle.

By telling Octavia what the spreadsheet should look like, or (worse) creating it for her, Spencer deprived her of the chance to figure it out and become a better marketer and a more skilled leader.

Life doesn't stand still. Getting better at solving today's problems doesn't prevent tomorrow's. Just the opposite, in fact: developing yourself means setting yourself up for bigger, more challenging problems in the future.

The next time there's a slightly different problem, Octavia will be equally dependent on Spencer to solve it for her. For her change to be sustainable, she needs to become future-proof.

You can help people develop resilience, as well as their ability to grow themselves, their leadership, and their organizations, by guiding and supporting them to intentionally and proactively use their difficulties to grow stronger.

At first, Daniel just wanted a gaming computer. He would have been fine—over the moon, actually—with just getting it delivered from Amazon. But that wasn't an option. So Daniel took advantage of the problem—I wasn't going to buy it for him, and he didn't have the money to buy it—to put himself in a much better position than just having a new computer.

After all, computers break. Suppose I had capitulated and bought him his dream machine. One day he kicks over the CPU during a particularly rousing game of Rocket Launcher and damages the motherboard. Now he's back where he was before, except much sadder.

Given how he's changed in the process of building his computer, that wouldn't be nearly as big a deal now. He knows how to find a motherboard online for under $150, and he's got the gear, know-how, and experience to earn that sum through a few hours of drone videography for nearby realtors.

In fact, given his new business, he can probably upgrade every part of his computer every few months—or even start another business building and selling gaming computers, or monetize a YouTube channel of his tutorials and reviews. In fact, now that he's tasted entrepreneurship, the sky's the limit.

In short, he dealt with a problem not just by solving it, but by solving it in a way that puts him in a much stronger, more capable position than if the problem had never presented itself.

★★★

We've identified how people change—through ownership, capability, emotional courage, and future-proofing. Now it's time to go from theory and concept into practice. Keep these "change powers" in mind as you dive into the Four Steps. You'll notice that each of the steps actualizes at least one—and often more—of these powers.

In the following group of chapters, we'll dive into Step 1 with a powerful mindset change to get you and the person you want to change on the same side, acting like partners. When you emerge from this step, the person you want to change will see you as an ally, not a critic, and you will be perfectly positioned to help them move forward in their change.

PART TWO

THE FOUR STEPS

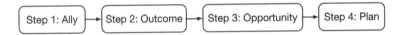

STEP ONE

SHIFT FROM CRITIC TO ALLY

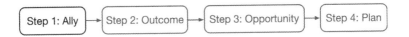

CHAPTER 7

BECOME AN ALLY

THE RAMONA PROBLEM

Ben leads a marketing team tasked with bringing a new software product to market. And he's frustrated.

Things aren't going well. The team is struggling to identify how the technology could be used and by whom. Without a clear use case—or customer base—the best technology in the world will go to waste, as will all the investment that went into creating it.

Morale is low. Solving this challenge is critical, and the team seems to be getting nowhere. The root of the problem appears to be Ramona, a digital strategist who has been complaining about their process for weeks. She's abrasive, rude, critical, and overbearing.

Over lunch, Ben complains to his colleague Dara. She wants to be a good friend. And she feels two conflicting impulses.

One is to cheer up Ben, to take his side: "That's so awful. Ramona sounds like a terrible person. Is there any way you can get rid of her?"

But Dara also wants to tell Ben how to solve the problem: "Look, it's your team. You set the rules. Just sit down and have it out with Ramona. That's your job."

Ask yourself: Is either of these approaches likely to help?

If Dara employs the first one, sympathy, she may help Ben feel better in the moment. It's always nice to be told that your perspective is valid. But it won't make him better. It won't help him become more skilled as a leader or more deft as a communicator. Dara would actually be Ben's enabler.

The second approach, advice, looks like it's designed to help Ben grow as a leader. But the underlying message is, "You're not doing this right. I know better." Ben will bristle, perhaps agree grudgingly, but almost certainly won't act on advice he didn't ask for.

Most people default to one or the other: collusion or criticism. They're both tempting, in different ways. When we take their side, we feel closer to them. Emotionally, it's a safe and satisfying move. A common enemy draws us together.

When we offer advice or criticize, we get a different kind of emotional payoff: We get to feel smart, competent, valuable, and superior—at their expense. And if we do it cleverly enough, we're blameless: "Hey, I'm only trying to help here."

But neither approach will help Ben get his team on track.

What Dara needs is a third option. One that maintains closeness and connection *and* that opens the door to actually solving the problem.

She needs an approach that both supports him in this moment and invites him to take ownership of the issue and grow his independent capability to deal with it. For that to happen, Ben needs to see Dara as a supporter, a helpful resource, and a thought partner. He needs to see her as his ally.

The effectiveness of the rest of the process depends on doing this well. After all, how you *start* something is often the most crucial step. It sets the tone. It determines your trajectory.

The right tone is to approach the person you want to help as an ally, rather than a critic.

When you approach someone as an ally, your strategies and tactics will be far more likely to succeed. Steps 2, 3, and 4 will show you what to do once you're an ally. Step 1 will show you how to establish that relationship from the start.

This can be surprisingly challenging.

Your drive to have the conversation in the first place may be laden with emotion. You want them to change (and maybe you've criticized them in the past) and they may desperately want to achieve a better outcome (and maybe they've tried and failed repeatedly, or they're scared or resistant to change). There's a lot at stake and a lot of feelings on the line.

Being a critic is seductively tempting. It feels good; you don't have to take any responsibility. You get to feel "better than" the person you're advising or criticizing.

But as we've seen, when we approach others from this place, we create resistance rather than willingness to change.

So how do you shift yourself from critic to ally? You do it, as you'll see in the next chapter, from the inside out.

CHAPTER 8

BE YOUR OWN ALLY FIRST

FIND YOUR POSITIVE INTENT

After Ben complained to Dara about Ramona, Dara returned to her office to think. She's glad that she bit her tongue and didn't give in to either impulse. She didn't take Ben's side against Ramona, and she didn't criticize his leadership. She listened and empathized with his frustration, and then they moved on, talking about other things: their kids, vacation plans, the new wellness program.

But the truth is, Dara didn't really move on. She's annoyed with Ben and how he's handling the situation. She wants to help him, but she also recognizes that the judgments she's harboring could get in the way.

She's right.

When you want to help someone else change, how you show up is a game changer. You need to start with yourself. Thankfully, there's a process for that: body, mind, emotions, intent—in that order.

BODY

The best, easiest, and most tangible and impactful place to start with yourself is physically.

Scan your body. Are your shoulders tense? Is your jaw clenched? Allow your muscles to relax. Take a couple of slow, deep breaths. Feel what it is like to be in your body. Notice any strong emotions, especially negative ones, and try to release them with your out-breaths. Just picture them floating out of your body and into the air as you exhale. You don't need to block off 30 minutes and put on trance music and sit in lotus position. You can do all this in half a minute, wherever you are. In fact, the goal *is* to be where you are—in the present.

MIND

After getting present in your body, go to your mind. Being present means not thinking about the past or future or about anything other than the conversation you're about to have. Take steps to eliminate or minimize distractions. Close your email and messaging apps, and silence notifications. Close any open mental loops that might bug you: capture the to-do's, ideas, and plans that are floating in your mind. Write them down so you can clear your mental RAM for other things. Gather your attention so it's fully available.

EMOTIONS

Once you've settled your body and your mind, it's time to go to your emotions. Ask yourself: "Am I frustrated, angry, disappointed, or worried about the other person?" Notice any judgments or criticism about them and their behavior. All of us are full of judgments and frustrations—having them isn't a problem. That's just how our minds and emotions work. But they won't help you show up as an ally. In order to be an ally, you need to move past them.

How can you overcome negative emotions and judgments? First, don't try to ignore or suppress your anger, frustration, annoyance, or disappointment. Unless you're the world's best actor, those attitudes will leak into your words, tone, facial expressions, and gestures.

Second, don't judge yourself for having judgments. Once you notice them, you may feel bad about having them. "I know I should be an ally, but I can't stop judging [that person]! Why am I so bad at this? What's wrong with me?"

Of course, criticizing yourself about being critical is simply continuing to be critical. It's the same ineffective strategy, just aimed at yourself. The key to becoming the other person's ally is to first become an ally to yourself, which means not beating yourself up.

Luckily, you don't have to get rid of any feelings in order to be an effective ally. There's another way: empathize with yourself. Explore the emotion with curiosity and find the positive intent behind it.

INTENT

Positive intent? How can there be positive intent behind anger or frustration?

The irony is that there is *always* positive intent behind every negative emotion. Think about it. You only get angry or frustrated or anxious or scared or sad when something you care about is at stake. The more you care, the more intensely you feel. The negative emotion, the one that leads you to act like a critic and stoke resentment, is actually a symptom of your caring, of your (misdirected) positive intent.

When you act from negative emotions, you are a critic. When you reconnect to what you care about, you shift into ally mode.

So get curious. Who—or what—do you care about enough that explains your strong negative emotions? The first thing that comes to mind might be an outcome or value that's important to you.

Get clear on that outcome or value. It might be tangible:

"I want to perform exhaustive due diligence before launching the platform to the business units" (for example, when the person you want to change has a habit of cutting corners).

It might also be an expression not of a specific goal or deliverable, but a value:

"I want to be treated with respect in this relationship" (for example, when the person you want to change is treating you poorly).

The useful move here is to expand your expression of that outcome or value to reflect your shared concern. How would this change benefit both of you?

You can identify your positive intent using this fill-in-the-blank formula:

The reason I'm _____ [negative emotion] *is because I care about* _____ [shared outcome or value].

Here are some examples, including the leap from self-focus to shared focus:

Self: "The reason I'm [frustrated with my chief marketing officer's lack of focus] is because I care about [the future of my company]."

Shared: "The reason I'm [frustrated with my chief marketing officer's lack of focus] is because I care about [our collective impact on the company]."

Self: "The reason I'm [angry at my boss's constant micromanaging] is because I care about [being left alone to get my work done]."

Shared: "The reason I'm [angry at my boss's constant micromanaging] is because I care about [having a productive relationship with my manager]."

And here's one that gets to the shared concern the first time:

"The reason I'm [disappointed in my son for getting poor grades] is because I care about [his success and happiness in life]."

Notice that the strength of your negative emotion is equal to your positive desire. See how your hurt is really a combination of your deep longing (or even love) and your perceived

helplessness. Depending on the situation and your relationship, you might care more about the person, or the outcome
you want them to achieve, or both. You might really want that
person to succeed, to be happy, to be healthy, or to feel confident. You might really need them to step up and contribute to
a project you're in charge of, to become the leader you need
them to be, to take schoolwork seriously, or to stop eating
junk food. Whatever the change, see how it integrates with
something the other person wants as well. That's how you can
approach them in ally mode.

So Dara checks in. What is she feeling toward Ben?

Frustration. So she digs deeper. What's frustrating her?
Despite his natural kindness, he's so conflict-averse that he'll
tolerate poor performance and a toxic environment rather
than speak up and address the issues directly. By being nice,
he's actually making himself and others miserable—and leading a team that's headed for failure.

She allows herself to feel all this fully, without pretending that she's not frustrated. Feeling into the frustration, she
realizes that she's more than frustrated—she's angry at Ben.
And then she asks herself: "What's behind my frustration
and anger?"

She discovers that she's frustrated and angry with Ben
because she cares. About him. About his team's success.
About what it will mean for his career. And—to be perfectly
honest—about what success or failure of this launch will
mean for her career and financial prospects. Her motives are
positive: She wants the best for him, and for herself, and for
their organization. And when she thinks about it, she's excited
about the potential for the software to improve people's lives.
It would be a shame to blow it.

★★★

Now it's your turn. Bring to mind a person in your life whom you'd like to help change. It could be someone from work, or a family member, or a friend. Prepare yourself for that conversation. Go through the body/mind/emotions/intent exercise. Before going to the next chapter, take a moment to identify your positive intent.

Once you've become your own ally—settling your body, mind, and emotions and connecting with the positive intent underlying your desire to change the other person—then you're ready to become their ally.

CHAPTER 9

THEN BE YOUR PARTNER'S ALLY

FIND THEIR POSITIVE INTENT

Now that Dara is in touch with her own positive intent, she thinks about Ben. Rather than seeing him as weak or cowardly or foolish, she asks, "What's the positive intent behind *his* behavior? What is he trying to accomplish?"

The move here is to put yourself in your partner's shoes. Imagine that you *are* them, acting the way they're acting, and there's a positive intent behind that behavior.

A Chief Marketing Officer might avoid tracking results because they're trying to protect their self-esteem in case the numbers don't meet expectations. Or because they've always been a blue-sky thinker and fear that managing to objectives will undermine their creativity.

A boss might micromanage because they want their team to succeed. Or because they think they're providing leadership and mentoring to their juniors. Or because they have a crystal-clear vision for a deliverable that they hold dear. Or some combination of all of those things.

A child might prioritize a social life over schoolwork because they want to be liked and esteemed by their peers

47

or because they don't feel good about their academic abilities and want to avoid feeling worthless.

When you identify a possible positive intent behind their dysfunctional behavior, you can soften your stance toward them and drop the judgments.

Moving from dysfunction to positive intent is a very simple shift. You don't need to be an expert on the various theories of human motivation to answer the question, "What's the positive intent behind their behavior?" All you need to know is that we all act with varying degrees of skill and clumsiness to help us get what we think we need. People with whom you're frustrated or angry are doing the very best they know how to meet some need. When you can plausibly identify what that might be, you automatically soften toward them.

Plausibly is the key word there. You don't have to "get it right." Your hypothesis might totally miss the mark, and that's OK. You're not trying to solve the riddle of their behavior at this point—that would just turn you into a dispenser of unwanted advice. Instead, you simply want to get yourself to a generous place, free from judgment, so you can approach them as a partner in getting what you both want.

You may come up with multiple theories: they're insecure, they're under a lot of pressure from their boss, or they're trying to inspire confidence in others. Keep those theories to yourself. They may come in handy during the Opportunity step, when you can offer them as trial balloons as you help your partner redefine the problem into one they can solve. Right now your goal is simply to approach them as an ally rather than a critic.

So how does Dara understand Ben's positive intent?

Dara thinks, "Ben just wants everyone to get along. He longs for a team where everyone feels valued and respected. He values peace and sees conflict as dangerous. That's why he doesn't address these interpersonal problems."

Flipping the switch from critic to ally is where a "miracle" occurs: when you step aside from the anger and criticism and blame, you suddenly drop your helplessness as well. As a partner, you have an entire new toolbox of powerful change techniques.

What does an ally look like? An ally is a resource, a thinking partner. As an ally, you show your partner that you believe in them and in their ability to handle the problem they're facing.

★★★

In the previous chapter, you connected with your positive intent for your partner. Now reflect on their positive intent: what positive outcome might they be going for, no matter how incomplete, clumsy, or counterproductive their efforts seem.

Give yourself time to shift from critic to ally, even if it takes days to flip the switch. Allow yourself time to feel all the feelings and find the positive intent and shared commitment that underpins them. Dara was right to walk away from the conversation and wait to re-engage until she could really show up as Ben's ally.

Once you feel centered and focused and are ready to approach the other person as a partner, you can move to the next step: getting their permission to have the change conversation.

CHAPTER 10

HOW TO GET PERMISSION TO HELP

SILVER PLATTER OPPORTUNITIES

Before trying to help someone, you need permission to have a conversation in the first place.

Remember: *People don't resist change. They resist being changed.*

When you begin helping someone who hasn't asked for help or agreed to it, they will feel that you're trying to change them. And they'll resist. Maybe not overtly, especially if you have power over them (you're their boss, for example). And you may not notice it right away—resistance often shows up only after the conversation, when they don't follow through on your suggestions.

When you ask for permission to help, on the other hand, you're handing them control. Whether or not they change is up to them, not you. When they say, "Yes, I'd like to have this conversation with you," that's the pivotal moment they begin to take accountability.

As managers, leaders, and parents we often try to "hold people accountable" after they've already failed to follow through. But that's too late. We need to help people "take accountability" in the first place *so that* they follow through.

That's why our first move is to ask permission to have the conversation.

You may be the world's greatest coach, consultant, adviser, strategist, or motivator, but if you don't receive permission from the person you want to help, you've doomed the effort to failure. On the flip side, you may be a beginner in the art of helping, but if you have their permission, your odds of success are good.

In the next chapter, you will learn how to get permission when you initiate the conversation, proactively approaching someone you want to help change.

First though, in this chapter, I want to help you recognize and capitalize on "Silver Platter" opportunities, moments that occur more frequently than you might realize and are easy to miss. These are moments when people come to you for help, for advice, or to complain. They are basically invitations to help them change. It's easier to get permission in these situations. You'll help people change earlier, and you'll avoid having to initiate the conversation in the first place.

THE PERMISSION FORMULA

The formula for obtaining permission when your partner asks for advice, wants you to do their job for them, or complains about a person or situation involves three steps:

1. Empathize with whatever requires empathy.[1]
2. Express confidence in their ability.
3. Offer to think it through with them.

---

[1]Download a bonus chapter on six techniques to express empathy in your conversations at BregmanPartners.com/change.

Let's start with the easiest situation: when they ask you for advice.

When They Ask You for Advice

Ludwig, a salesperson, has been working to land a lucrative contract with a prospect, Symphony Corp. He goes to his manager, Dorothea, for advice.

Let's see how Dorothea can get permission to help Ludwig solve his problem in a way that grows his ownership and independent capability. She begins with empathy, and then—because he's already come to her for help—confirms permission to help in the way that she wants to help.

Do:

LUDWIG: What should I include in my presentation to Symphony's executive team next week? It's a big one!

DOROTHEA: Yeah, this is a big one. [*Empathy*] Great job on that, by the way. [*Confidence*] Let's think this through together, OK? [*Think together*]

Dorothea garners permission to help Ludwig change by going through the three-part formula described above.

When They Want You to Do It for Them

Now let's look at a second situation, where the person asks you to do something that they can and should do for themselves. If solving their problem for them is not your job, and in fact doing so routinely will turn you into a bottleneck, use the permission formula.

Do:

LUDWIG: Hey, I've just gotten a meeting with Symphony's executive team, and they asked for a custom presentation. I really want it to be perfect. Could you put something together for me?

DOROTHEA: This is a big opportunity and I really appreciate you wanting it to be perfect. [*Empathy*] I also really believe in you—which is how you've gotten this far with them and why you're pitching it. [*Confidence*] Putting together these custom presentations will be important for you moving forward. Can we think through together how to approach this one? [*Think together*]

As Ludwig's manager, Dorothea can be explicit about her intent to help him develop his professional skill set. If this conversation were between two colleagues, it might not be appropriate to tell Ludwig that he will need to develop this skill for his future success. A colleague can express confidence in a different way than a manager: "Congrats, Ludwig! So great that you got this. They obviously have a lot of confidence in you. Let's think it through together."

Ludwig will either say, "Yes," in which case you're off to the races, or "No" if he doesn't want help thinking about it but wants her to tell him exactly what to do. In the latter case, it's important for Dorothea to know, and establish, her boundary. Dorothea can refuse permission to take over parts of Ludwig's job.

Do:

LUDWIG: I really don't know how to prepare the presentation.

DOROTHEA: I know it's new for you. Let's think about it together.

Dorothea is firm about two things: she's not going to do it, and she has faith that Ludwig can. Those are her tools to get permission to have the helping conversation.

We say "Yes" to doing things for other people because setting a boundary by saying "No" can feel so uncomfortable. Harder in the moment, but better for everyone in the long run, is for you to set the boundary up front.

Do:

BEN: Hey, Dara, my team is struggling and I think Ramona is the issue. She's so bossy. Since you know her well, can you talk to her?

DARA: I'm sorry to hear that. Leading teams can be so hard. [*Empathy*] I honestly think it will be useful for you to develop your relationship with her. And I know you can. [*Confidence*] I think the feedback should come from you. Can we think through the situation? [*Think together*]

BEN: Yeah, that would be helpful. Thanks.

Of course, Ben might not agree right away, even after receiving empathy and confidence. He might continue to push back, lobbying for his original request.

Do:

BEN: I'd really rather you do it.

DARA: I'm sure. [*Said with a smile*] I would too if I were you. I'm not comfortable doing it, though. But can I help you think through the situation?

WHEN THEY COMPLAIN TO YOU

It would be nice if everyone approached us directly for guidance, advice, or help. In those cases, at the very least, they want the problem solved. Unfortunately, it's much more common for people to initiate a conversation with you by complaining. By complaining I mean expressing discontent, frustration, or annoyance without intending to do anything about it.

Which is fine and very human.

All of us complain to some degree. And sometimes complaining is nothing more than letting off steam. It can feel good—and it's important at times—to get things off our chest. To complain because we want someone to validate our experience.

Often though, people in our lives complain to us about problems that they could deal with, should deal with, and want to have handled. Yet they don't do anything about those problems—except complain. They typically complain about other people. Sometimes they complain about the work, but that's usually a proxy for complaining about the people who created the work, people who aren't holding up their end of the work, or people who are holding them accountable for the work.

When someone complains repeatedly, they're demonstrating a lack of accountability. So our job, if we want to help them, is to shift them from complaining to solving. From victimhood to agency.

Even then, we should follow the permission formula. Empathy is the best first move to shift the other person to problem solving.

Let's say Ben isn't asking Dara to intervene, and he's not asking for advice or help. He's just venting—which is to say, complaining.

Don't:

BEN: Ramona just torpedoed our meeting with the
          digital marketing agency. She treated them like
          3-year-olds.

DARA: I get it. But maybe your management style is the
          root of the problem.

BEN: [*Sweaty, defensive face; thinking: "Last time I come to
          YOU with a problem."*]

Dara's impression could be correct: Ben might be mismanaging his team. She might even have corroborating feedback from his team members. The problem is, even if she's right, even if Ben will have to accept that reality in order to improve his performance, she's jumping the gun by rushing to that statement.

Another mistake would be to agree with the complaint.

Don't:

BEN:	Hey, Dara, my team is struggling and I think Ramona is the issue. She's so bossy. Since you know her well, can you talk to her?
DARA:	Yeah, Ramona is a pain to work with. Always has been.

Empathy and agreement are not the same. Empathy does not require agreement. You can and should empathize without adopting or agreeing with their perspective.

Still, Dara has to earn the right to explore Ben's contribution to the problem by *understanding* his perspective.

Do:

BEN:	Ramona is bossing everyone on the team. She's so annoying, especially because she's the one with the least experience.
DARA:	That sounds tough. [*Empathy*]
BEN:	Yeah, it is. Everyone's spending so much time defending their turf that we're not accomplishing our mission. It's infuriating.
DARA:	Sounds like it's a larger dynamic than just Ramona. And it's something I know you can handle as the team leader. [*Confidence*] Want to think about the situation together? [*Think together*]
BEN:	Yeah, that would be great. Thanks.

When you look at the preceding dialogue, you might think that Dara's initial response ("That sounds tough") is annoyingly obvious. The truth is, simple affirmations of a person's feelings communicate caring in a way that little else does. Even reflecting back Dan's complaint by repeating it more or less verbatim (Dara: "That sounds so annoying.") will work. It just feels good to be seen and heard and acknowledged without judgment.

Alternately, Dara can show empathy by admitting that she's had the same problems in the past.

Do:

BEN: Other team members are fed up with Ramona's rudeness. I've never seen morale so low. And it doesn't help that we still don't have a use case to build a marketing campaign on.

DARA: That's hard. I've had similar struggles with teams in the past. Do you want to think about this together?

In the next chapter, we'll explore how to get permission when our partner is not coming to us for help at all. In this situation, we want to help them even though they haven't asked for it.

CHAPTER 11

HOW TO INITIATE THE CONVERSATION

DO YOU HAVE A MINUTE?

The dialogues up to this point represent situations where the other person has given you an opening to ask for permission. Either they have asked for advice, or help, or complained about a problem verbally, or they have demonstrated unhappiness or struggled in a way that invited empathy.

But how can you get permission when you're the one initiating the conversation?

The simple answer is to lead with the punchline. And in this case, the punchline is your positive intention: what you want to achieve or get. Think back to the preparation you did in identifying your intention for the conversation (from Chapter 10). Request permission by leading with that outcome or value, using the following formula:

"Hey, do you have a minute to talk? I want _____ [outcome or value]. *I'd like to talk with you about what I think is getting in the way. Would you be willing to be in this conversation with me?"*

Too often, we try to "soften the blow" or get to the point indirectly.

Don't:

BEN: Hey, Ramona, do you have a minute?

RAMONA: Yeah, sure.

BEN: You did a great job setting up the dummy table for lifetime customer value.

RAMONA: Thanks.

BEN: [*Awkwardly*] I did want to mention one thing, though . . .

RAMONA: [*Heart starting to pound; face flushing*] Yeah?

The understandable (but misguided) idea is that by starting with something positive, Ben has established rapport that will make it easier to talk about the problem. But what actually has happened is that Ramona no longer cares about the compliment, because she's just received a danger signal from the environment. It's like you're driving down the road, enjoying a song on the radio, and all of a sudden you hear a siren and see flashing red and blue lights behind you.

At that point, who cares about the song?

That's not to say that you should begin by blurting out the problem, either.

Don't:

BEN: Hey, Ramona, you're being rude, bossy, and overly aggressive in our team meetings.

RAMONA: I'm sorry if you guys can't handle the truth. Geez.

Instead, start by letting the other person know that you'd like to talk with them, and describe your intention for the conversation. This sets up the rest of the conversation for success. Rather than beginning with feedback, which is about the past, and typically negative, begin by requesting to talk about a future that you want, and invite them to partner with you.

Do:

BEN: Hey, Ramona, do you have a minute to talk?

RAMONA: Yeah, sure.

BEN: I'd like to improve the performance of our team, and I think your contributions could be key. I'd like to talk with you about what's getting in the way.

If they cannot or do not want to talk now, that's fine. Get permission to schedule the conversation at a later time.

Do:

BEN: Hey, Ramona, do you have a minute to talk?

RAMONA: Not really. What's up?

BEN: I want our team to do better, and I'd like to talk with you about what's getting in the way. If you're willing to have that conversation with me, can we schedule it?

You may be thinking at this point, "Wait a minute—I thought we were supposed to start with empathy. Now you're telling me to start with the punchline. Which is it?"

Great question!

You empathize only in response to something the other person has expressed. If, on the other hand, you are initiating the conversation—in other words, the other person hasn't said anything yet—then you've got nothing to empathize with.

So where does empathy come in? When you're initiating the conversation, you start by stating your desired outcome and ask if they are willing to talk about what's getting in the way of that outcome. If they say "Yes," move on to Step 2.

Now, there is a chance—it's likely even—that the other person will get defensive. They'll brace themselves for criticism ("Ben obviously thinks *I'm* the problem") and put up a wall of resistance.

You have two moves here. First, if possible, acknowledge that the problem is bigger than they are. You should take personal responsibility for whatever you can. By being vulnerable, you can help them drop their self-protective impulses as well.

Do:

BEN: I'd like to improve the performance of our team, and I think your contributions could be key. I'd like to talk with you about what's getting in the way.

RAMONA: You mean how *I'm* getting in the way?

BEN: I think you have really good points to make, and they're not being received by the group, and I'd like to work with you to change that. I think part of that is the team. And I've played a part too—I've seen the ways I shut you down, and I apologize. I'm sorry I've done that. I want to change how I show up in our meetings. And I also think there are things you can do and say differently that will help you show up more effectively so that it will be more likely that you have the impact on the team that you intend. I'd really like to look at how each of us could do things differently to get to a high-performing team. Are you willing to be in that conversation with me?

Second, empathize with whatever you can.

Do:

RAMONA: I feel like I can't say anything without you guys just clamming up. And we have real issues to deal with. I'm frustrated because I feel like I have to end up fighting everyone—the marketing people, the team, you—to get anything done. It's

	really annoying, especially when everyone makes me out to be the villain here.

BEN: That sounds really rough. I know what it's like to not be heard or taken seriously, and I'm sorry that's been your experience. And I agree—you raise really good points, and they aren't getting heard, and we're all losing. I really want to figure out how to fix this—how you, I, and the team can all do things differently to get to a high-performing team where you're contributing fully.

RAMONA: Well, I do too. I'm really tired with how things have been going.

Again, empathy doesn't necessarily mean agreement. You can—and should—empathize without taking sides.

INITIATING THE CONVERSATION WITH A COLLEAGUE

Initiating a change conversation is probably the hardest part of the Four Steps. It's hard for Ben, even though as Ramona's boss he has the right and responsibility to deal with the situation.

It's even harder when you don't have that right and responsibility. At work, you aren't obligated to try to change people who don't report to you. So how do you approach colleagues who aren't pulling their weight, and you, along with your team and organization, are paying the price?

Don't lead with an accusation or anything that will trigger defensiveness.

Don't:

SELENA: Hey, Darshana. I feel like I'm doing all the work on the onboarding handbook, and it's not fair. Can we talk about it?

As always, do your internal preparation. Remind yourself of your positive intent. What value is important to you here? Take time to think of some generous interpretations of your colleague's behavior. If they weren't lazy and unmotivated, what else could explain the behavior? If they didn't hate you, why might they have been acting that way? Picture what you want for them, and for both of you.

You can then initiate the request for permission by first asking to talk about the context in which the problem is occurring. Keep it neutral. The neutral context in this example is the onboarding handbook. In another situation, it might be "our weekly meetings" or "the hiring process" or "the staff refrigerator." There's nothing inherently good or bad about handbooks or processes or refrigerators.

Next, tell them that you're struggling, or having a problem, or finding something difficult or challenging. This isn't their problem—it's yours. And using a word like *struggling*, if it's true, conveys some vulnerability on your part. You need their help with your problem. You're enlisting their generosity and goodwill. Finally, explicitly request their help. Luckily, it's quicker to do than to describe.

Do:

SELENA: Can we talk about the onboarding handbook for a second? I'm struggling with how we're working together on it, and I'd love your help.

DARSHANA: Yes. What's the problem?

At that point, don't jump into blame. They haven't agreed to be changed—just to hear about your problem. So now you have to describe the problem in a way that reflects your most generous interpretation of their behavior.

Don't:

SELENA: The problem is, you're not doing what you say you're going to do. We agreed that you were going to draft chapters 2 and 3, and I was going to draft chapters 5 and 6. But when we met, you hadn't done your chapters and were expecting me to draft them for you in that meeting. I want you to take your commitments more seriously!

By leading with criticism ("you're not doing what you said you were going to do"), Selena puts Darshana on the defensive. Now she's likely to push back:

DARSHANA: I take my commitments very seriously. But this project is total BS. I've been here longer than you—we never end up using documents like this. It's a total waste of time, and you may not realize it, but I'm in up to my eyeballs leading the search committee for the new head of HR since Lionel quit last month.

Do:

SELENA: I feel like we're having an issue with how we're communicating about the work. For example, the last couple of meetings I thought we had divided up the work so that I was going to draft a couple of chapters and you were going to draft a couple of chapters. But when we met, you hadn't drafted yours, and we spent the meeting working on those chapters together. And honestly, it didn't feel great. And what I really want is for us to have a great working relationship and to be really clear about what each of us is going to accomplish.

DARSHANA: Well, I want that too. I just thought that it would end up being more efficient to work on it together, rather than me writing and you totally rewriting it later.

SELENA: I see where you're coming from. And I didn't
             realize that's what you were thinking. I obvi-
             ously want to get this done well, and I also value
             our relationship. So can we talk about creating a
             communication system and workflow that works
             for both of us?

DARSHANA: Yes, let's.

INITIATING THE CONVERSATION WHEN IT'S
PURELY PERSONAL

The trickiest place to initiate a change conversation may be
in your personal life, with family and friends who may feel
that how they live their lives is "none of your business."

Sometimes, of course, it *is* your business. When the situation
directly involves your relationship—they're using hurtful language, or giving you the silent treatment, or belittling you in
front of the kids—you can use the same formula as you'd use
with a colleague. Describe the neutral context, say what you're
struggling with, and ask for their help. If they agree to that, share
your experience without blaming, and say what you want instead.

Do:

ELAINE: Hey, Julia, can I talk to you about dinnertime?
             I'm struggling with how it's going, and I'd love
             your help.

JULIA: Yeah, what's the problem?

ELAINE: I look forward to seeing you and spending time
             with you after we've both been working all day,
             and lately you've been texting and scrolling dur-
             ing our dinners. I'm feeling disconnected from
             you and really miss our old routine where we
             really made time for each other. Could we talk
             about how to get back to something like that?

JULIA: Well, you know my mother's been in and out of the hospital, and dinnertime is the first time during the day that I can talk with my sister about what's going on. And honestly, I'm fried by the time I come home, and Instagram relaxes me. And it's not like you've been a treat to be around the last couple of months, since you hurt your knee and stopped running.

At first glance, it may feel like this didn't go so well. Julia is venting and being defensive. But, actually, Julia's response isn't just fine; it's progress.

Julia's venting is a way of connecting, and Elaine's best next move is to listen and empathize. It may not be easy for her, but remember what she wants: connection. Instead of texting or scrolling on Instagram, Julia is sharing her feelings and frustrations.

The conversation isn't done—it's just getting started—but what's most important is that they're in it.

INITIATING THE CONVERSATION WHEN IT'S NONE OF YOUR BUSINESS

Sometimes the other person's behavior is none of your business, at least technically. Maybe you want to talk to your neighbors about the fact that their kid doesn't wear a bike helmet. Perhaps your running buddy has just been diagnosed with high blood pressure and still orders greasy, salty food when you grab lunch together. Maybe your adult child is in a toxic relationship, and you hate seeing them unhappy, and you want to tell them to stand up for themselves and set clear boundaries. How do you initiate a change conversation when you could be perceived as "meddling"?

First, get really, *really* clear on your positive intent. Recognize the ways in which you had been approaching them as a critic rather than an ally:

"What kind of parent lets their kid ride in the street without a helmet?"

"Sal knows better than to eat cheeseburgers and dirty fries! And with three young kids at home—he's so irresponsible!"

"What does Dylan see in that creep anyway? I would have broken it off months ago!"

You have to drop any traces of superiority—knowing better or being more responsible. Your approach in a situation like that must convey your deep caring, a clear acknowledgment that this isn't your business, and an honest expression of your own vulnerability in the face of your fears for them. If you have lost someone to traumatic brain injury, or cardiovascular disease, or addiction, you can share that—not to make this "all about you," but to make it clear that you're not approaching from a position of superiority.

The hardest case is when you've messed this up in the past. For example, you've been nagging your brother about his terrible diet for the past 20 years, sending him diet books and links to TED talks and documentaries about morbidly obese people who are now running ultramarathons.

Before you can use any of the strategies in this book, you're going to have to undig that hole—because your brother is just waiting for your next sermon. Even if you say nothing when you visit, he'll interpret that silence as judgment about the contents of his fridge and pantry. You've got to break his stereotype of you before he'll listen to a word you say.

One way to do this is to simply stop trying to change him, at least for a while. If he orders cheesecake, just let him enjoy it.

But don't stop there. Instead, own what you can about your past behavior. Don't even justify it by saying how much you care or how worried you are. Simply acknowledge that you've been strident, probably annoying, and that you're sorry. Tell him that you want to stop treating him like a child, and ask him to let you know when you slip up. You can even check in periodically—"How'm I doing?"—as a way of spotlighting your own change. When you own your actions and apologize, that's a very strong move. By stepping back, you make room for him to step forward and actually ask for your help.

"That's all right. I know you have my best interests at heart. Truth is, I'm scared about my health. My last checkup was pretty bad."

Now they're complaining, which is your opening to say, "Would you like to think this through together?"

Note that I didn't tell you to say, "Are you finally ready to listen to the advice I've been shouting into the wind for years?"

You're not going to jump in with advice. Instead, you'll move on to Step 2, and talk with them about what they want to happen. Rather than trying to drag them somewhere (to your diet, your doctor's website, your meditation app), you're guiding them to drive their own change. The more they feel in control, and the less you do, the more likely they'll develop ownership and grow their independent capability.

We've now covered how to ask for permission in the most common situations. In the next chapter, let's look at a power dynamic that might overlap any of these situations: getting permission when you're the boss.

CHAPTER 12

DON'T RELY ON YOUR POSITION OF POWER

ARE YOU WILLING TO TRY SOMETHING?

When you're the boss and technically don't need your employees' permission to offer guidance, advice, and help, you should still get it. As we've seen, presuming permission creates resistance by degrading their ownership over the change, reducing the likelihood that they'll follow through.

And, truth be told, you generally have way less positional power than you think. Employees can often ignore you without consequences. Or they can leave. And they can do the bare minimum to avoid getting fired.

Don't (Permission assumed):

LAMONT (FRED'S EMPLOYEE):   Aisha hasn't given me her reports yet, so I can't get you the white paper by the Friday deadline.

FRED (LAMONT'S BOSS): Let's talk about how you can be clearer in setting expectations.

LAMONT: OK, sure. [*The forced yes*]

Do (Permission sought):

LAMONT: Aisha hasn't given me her reports yet, so I can't get you the white paper by the Friday deadline.

FRED: Do you want to think this through together?

LAMONT: [*Relieved*] Yes, that would be great. [*True permission*]

What if you ask permission and don't get it? You are still accountable for your employees' outcomes. If you're a manager, you suffer if your employees aren't appropriately productive or collaborative.

So what's the way out?

HOW TO USE POSITIONAL POWER IN THE WORKPLACE

When you're the boss, you have positional power—people are supposed to listen to you because you're the boss. But wielding that power unskillfully reduces their ownership and erodes their accountability.

So how do you use your power skillfully? Clearly state your expectations about outcomes, without ego and without drama.

Don't:

FRED: Do you want to think this through together?

LAMONT: No, there's nothing I can do here. She's the bottleneck.

FRED: Well, that's not how I see it. [*Annoyed*] Are you sure she understands your expectations? [*Starts problem solving without permission*]

LAMONT: [*Bristles*] Yes, I was very clear. [*Resisting; not giving permission to explore solutions*]

Do:

LAMONT: Aisha hasn't given me her reports yet, so I can't get you the white paper by the Friday deadline.

FRED: I'm sorry you're struggling with Aisha. That said, I still expect the white paper by Friday. Do you want to think through how to approach Aisha?

When you deliver your expectations, your tone of voice is crucial. You should not be annoyed, whiny, or judgmental. You have actual power here, and you should use it without fanfare or apology—simply state the facts. You have the right to set and enforce clear expectations. More than your right, it's your responsibility as a boss. Think about bosses you've had who weren't good at clearly stating their expectations. I'm guessing they weren't very effective or great to work with.

What if your employee digs in their heels and still refuses your offer of help? When someone reports to you, you need their permission to *help* them do their job. But you do not need their permission to hold them accountable.

Do:

LAMONT: There's no point brainstorming this.

FRED: OK, I'm sure you'll figure it out. I still need to see the white paper from you by Friday.

LAMONT: I just explained that it's out of my hands. I can't get it to you on Friday.

FRED: I understand that you are struggling with Aisha. That said, I expect you to honor your commitments to me. The offer stands: I'm happy to think it through with you. Otherwise, I have confidence that you will figure it out on your own.

When Alan Mulally became CEO of Ford Motor Company in 2006, the company was in trouble: staggering annual losses, poor-quality products, and low morale. Within a few years, Ford was resurgent: profitable, making great vehicles, and humming with purpose. It was the only U.S. auto company not to declare bankruptcy during the 2008–2009 recession. And this all happened with essentially the same leadership team. How did Mulally manage to turn around a global corporation with hundreds of thousands of employees, all of whom had to change their behaviors to make it happen?

As Mulally tells the story, his most important tool was accountability. He didn't get mad, and he didn't criticize anyone's behavior. He simply expressed consequences. The message to someone who wasn't doing what they were supposed to do: "Your behavior is perfectly fine. Just not here." They were invited to change, or leave.

Almost all of them stayed. Mulally turned around Ford without turning over its leadership. They changed. He changed them.

When you approach your employees in this way, it's rare that they'll refuse your offer to help. You don't have to practice awkward phrases in front of the mirror. Simple questions do the trick:

"Do you want to think this through together?"

"Do you want some help?"

"Do you want to hear my thoughts?"

"Are you willing to try something?"

No matter your position or power in the relationship, asking permission is the key first move to becoming an ally with the person you're wanting to help change. It gives them the choice, power, and ownership that's necessary for them to take the next step.

As you gain their permission, there are a number of possible pitfalls you may encounter. Recognizing and avoiding them is the subject of the next chapter.

CHAPTER 13

STAY ON TRACK

PITFALLS TO AVOID

Now that you know the "moves" to get permission, let's look at some pitfalls to avoid.

GETTING STUCK IN A COMPLAINT/ EMPATHY LOOP

Receiving empathy feels good. Most people don't get to experience it all that often. So when you empathize with a complaint, or a negative emotion, you may trigger another complaint or statement of victimhood.

Don't:

HARLAN: A number of people expressed concern to me about how you spoke to Ivy in the kick-off meeting.

ANGELO: Did you know that she tried to go behind my back and pitch a radio campaign?

HARLAN: I didn't know—I'm sorry.

ANGELO:	Yeah, thank you. She kneecaps me every chance she gets.
HARLAN:	You've been struggling with this for a while, sounds like.
ANGELO:	It's miserable working with her.
HARLAN:	You sound frustrated.
ANGELO:	Whatever I do, she either sabotages or tries to take credit.

Harlan's empathy ("I didn't know—I'm sorry.") triggered more complaining. Harlan continued to empathize with each negative statement, eliciting more and more complaints without being helpful at all. Avoid the complaint/empathy loop by refusing to take the bait after the second complaint. Instead, pivot to problem solving.

Do:

| ANGELO: | Yeah, thank you. She kneecaps me every chance she gets. |
| HARLAN: | Can I help you think through how to handle the situation to get a positive resolution—or at least one that doesn't leave you looking bad? |

FORCING A YES

Here's the thing about asking for permission: You must be 100 percent OK with not getting it—especially when you have power over them.

If the people you are trying to get permission from think your question is disingenuous—if they believe your question is rhetorical and demands their agreement—their agreement will also be disingenuous. They'll give you an external, fake "Yes," while stubbornly holding on to their internal, resistant "No way."

Don't:

LAMONT: Aisha hasn't given me her reports yet, so I can't get you the white paper by Friday.

FRED: Do you just want to complain about it, or do you want to fix it?

The forced yes is the same as not getting permission at all. It may be worse, because the other person now believes this unpleasant conversation is partly their fault. Now they're annoyed at themselves, and definitely at you.

Which means that—and here's the hard part—you may need to take *no* for an answer. Remember, they will change when they choose to change.

What makes this hard is that no matter what, if you are the boss and you say, "Would you like to think this through?" they may feel no choice but to say "Yes"—which makes it all the more important to be genuine when you ask for permission. Then you will reinforce their ownership as you continue through Steps 2, 3, and 4 and they realize that the choice of how to move forward is entirely theirs.

The counterintuitive thing is that often, over time, when they recognize that you respect their right to say "No," eventually they use that power to say "Yes." Their "No" is often about power and control. Give it to them, and then they are free to choose "Yes"—when they're ready.

REFUSING TO TAKE "NO" FOR AN ANSWER

If you fail to get the permission you're after, you might be tempted to shift to a more "hardball" tactic. Don't. It will backfire.

So, before you engage in asking permission, ask yourself two questions:

"Am I genuinely curious about whether they want help with this issue?"

"Am I willing to take 'No' for an answer?"

If you can't honestly answer "Yes" to both questions, then pause before you engage. As you think about their issue, notice your thoughts. Notice your emotions around those thoughts. Notice any physical sensations that accompany the emotions and thoughts. If these thoughts, emotions, and sensations are intense and/or unpleasant, that may be a signal that you may want this change more than they do. Your words, no matter how skillfully you stick to the script, will convey this demand.

And they will resist it.

RUSHING

Don't be in a rush for someone to change. As psychotherapist Fritz Perls said, "Don't push the river; it flows by itself." People move and change in their own time.

That said, you can influence their timeline in either direction: Pushing too hard will slow them down by generating resistance or stopping them outright. And creating the conditions in which they feel safe enough to challenge their own status quo will encourage their forward momentum.

If someone is about to do immediate harm to themselves or someone else (your employee is about to tell a dirty joke to the CEO, or your child is about to run into a busy street, or your child is about to tell a dirty joke to the CEO), then acting with urgency is the exact right thing to do.

But in most cases, there's no immediate danger and when you act as though there is, it's a sign that their issue has triggered one of yours. What's appropriate here is to stand down.

How can you tell when you're acting from your own "triggered" place rather than as a balanced, measured, mature adult? Any bout of uncontrolled (or barely controlled) anger on your part is a tell-tale sign. You'll notice energy building inside you that feels almost impossible to contain.

Don't:

CARL: They complain that other people aren't giving them what they need. It's total buck-passing.

LIZ: Carl, do you realize how ridiculous you sound?! You're doing the exact same thing!

As in this example, questions that are not really questions also are a clue that you're triggered. When you feel that energy—when it's about you, and not them—they'll know it and you'll stop being effective. At that point, take a breath and give *yourself* a timeout.

There's always tomorrow.

Their change is about them. It has to be their choice. Your patience creates the space for them to choose. Remember, people don't resist change; they resist *being* changed.

BECOMING DEFENSIVE

Sometimes, despite our best efforts, people get defensive when we try to help them, which can trigger our defensiveness in response. At times they even express defensiveness at our attempts at empathy.

Don't:

CARL: My team members complain that other people aren't giving them what they need. It's total buck-passing.

LIZ: That's frustrating. I've led teams where that was happening. Maybe we can figure something out together?

CARL: They don't act like professionals. There's nothing I can do.

LIZ: Well, if you won't look at your own behavior here, I can't help you.

It would be natural for Liz to react defensively here. She's doing her best to help, and Carl is refusing to take any responsibility for his team's performance. Instead, reach once again for empathy. Be present to what they're expressing.

Do:

CARL: They don't act like professionals. There's nothing I can do.

LIZ: I can see how frustrating that is. I have a few thoughts—let me know if you want to discuss it.

Getting permission is the most important part of helping people change. Even though there is a lot to consider, the actual practice of requesting permission usually takes just a few seconds.

Once you have received genuine permission, whether explicit or implicit, you can move to Step 2: Identify an Energizing Outcome.

STEP 2

IDENTIFY AN ENERGIZING OUTCOME

CHAPTER 14

PROBLEMS ARE SIGNPOSTS POINTING TO ENERGIZING OUTCOMES

NO MORE CODE, NO MORE BUGS

Back to Ben and Dara.

Ben said, "Yes," he'd really appreciate Dara's help in thinking through the Ramona problem. And Dara is eager to roll up her sleeves. After all, she's got a lot of experience building and managing teams, along with some hard-won wisdom about how to work with aggressive know-it-alls like Ramona. How she longs to share it with Ben! But she knows that doing so now would be a mistake.

Once you receive permission to help, you'll be tempted to jump in—to share advice, brainstorm solutions, and help your partner solve their problem. I know it's tempting, but don't do it—not yet.

In fact, the problem is actually a distraction from what's really important, from what will really make a difference in their life.

This is the crucial insight I want to impart in Step 2:

Problems (what we *don't* want) are signposts pointing to energizing outcomes (what we *do* want).

If we solve their problem before identifying their energizing outcome, they will not be much better off than they were before.

Let's look at some ridiculous examples that make the point. In the children's book *Thank You, Amelia Bedelia*, the main character removes stains from her employer's dress by cutting the stains out with scissors. No more stains—problem solved!

In the HBO comedy series *Silicon Valley*, a harried coder tasks his Artificial Intelligence program with identifying and fixing the bugs in their mission-critical software. The AI "solves" the bug problem, as efficiently as possible, by deleting all the code, acting like a high-tech Amelia Bedelia. No more code, no more bugs. And just to drive home the point, in the same episode the AI orders four thousand pounds of meat after being tasked with finding cheap hamburgers for lunch.

OK, those stories are funny (to kids and coders, anyway), but what do they have to do with real life? Well, consider Pavel, head of sales. He's frustrated at his team's long and unproductive sales meetings. The obvious solution is to shorten the meetings. So he insists that the meetings run no longer than 23 minutes, and to encourage compliance, he removes the chairs from the conference room.

Problem solved, right? Sure, the meetings are now much shorter. But if nothing else changes, the meetings are still inefficient and unproductive, just shorter—which means that now they're getting even less done in the meetings than before.

And here's another one: Elaine is frustrated that her wife, Julia, is constantly on her phone during dinner, scrolling through videos and responding to Instagram comments. Elaine insists they put their phones in a drawer while eating. Julia complies, but is sullen and distant during the meal. She's not on her phone (problem solved), but neither spouse is happy or feels satisfied.

What's missing in these stories? Why is solving the problem so unsatisfactory?

Each case misses the significance of the problem (something you don't want) as a signpost pointing toward something positive (something you do want). Amelia Bedelia's mandate was a clean and wearable dress. In *Silicon Valley*, the desired outcome of the AI program was clean code that worked. Pavel doesn't want just shorter meetings, but productive and efficient ones. And Elaine doesn't just want a phone-free dinner; she wants to connect with Julia.

In other words, problems are data that something in your life is misaligned with an outcome that's important to you. The problem is useful because it points you to what matters. It's actually the whole point of trying to solve the problem. Compare "I want you to put your phone down" (solve the problem) to "I want to connect with you" (outcome). Julia could "solve" the problem by putting her phone down and finishing dinner in five minutes, eating so quickly that there's no room to talk—not an improvement.

An outcome that is **positive**, **clear**, and **meaningful** is inspiring and exciting. It points to an exact destination. You can create milestones based on that destination. And you can adapt strategies based on feedback related to that destination.

Here's a real-life example of the guiding power of outcome.

A friend of mine confessed that he had made a huge mistake on a spreadsheet, one that had cost his company a lot of money. He was wondering whether to tell his boss about it. "I could probably get away with it. She might never find out."

Like the broken record I can be (and hopefully you will be too), I asked, "What's the outcome you're going for?"

He replied, "I want my boss to trust me with important and complex work." That's positive, clear, and meaningful.

The second he spoke, he knew that he had to come clean. The issue wasn't getting away with it; this was a trusted relationship. And he knew that hiding something this important from his boss would create the opposite of trust. By admitting the error, he would in fact demonstrate his integrity.

Another example: A client runs a division of a company with staff all over the world and was about to launch a weekly web meeting for the division. She had been reading about all the creative ways businesses are using group video conferencing and had literally hundreds of ideas for activities and formats. She asked my advice about how she should use that hour-long weekly meeting. Can you guess what I said in reply?

"So, what's the outcome you're going for?"

Why? Because there's no "right" answer to a problem in the absence of outcome. Did she want her team members to become more comfortable with each other? To align their actions around a common focus and goal? To use the video platform more effectively?

Each of those outcomes would suggest a different strategy. Once she knows what she's going for, she can begin to weigh options in terms of which ones will get her to that outcome.

Trying to solve a problem without stating the desired outcome is like entering "Anywhere but here" in your GPS.

On the other hand, using that problem to identify an energizing outcome is like typing an actual address. In this step—Step 2—you're going to guide your partner to translate their problem into an energizing outcome.

Let's see how this plays out in a real conversation. So far in our story, Ben has given Dara permission to think through the Ramona issue with him. Watch, in the dialogue below, how Dara helps him identify his energizing outcome.

BEN: Thanks for thinking about this with me. Ramona—
         who you know is a member of the team like every-
         one else—is super bossy and the rest of the team is
         struggling with it.

DARA: Got it. What's the outcome you want here?

BEN: I want Ramona to stop bossing people around.

DARA: What would you like her to be doing instead?

BEN: Be collaborative and respectful.

DARA: What would that look like?

BEN: She'd act like a colleague. An equal. A part of the team.

DARA: And what would *that* look like? What would she be
         saying or doing?

BEN: She'd ask questions rather than tell everyone what to
         do. She would listen with real curiosity. She'd make
         suggestions that engage people rather than make
         them defensive.

DARA: What would that give you?

BEN: That would give me a functional team. That would
         create an environment where people feel safe to
         share what they're thinking.

DARA: Tell me what a functional team would look like.

BEN: We'd stop getting in each other's way.

DARA: Tell me more. What would people be doing
         or saying?

BEN: Well, they'd stop complaining about each other, for
         one thing.

DARA: [*Noticing that Ben has gone negative again*] Great. And
         as a functional team, what would they do instead of
         complaining?

BEN: They'd take responsibility for their deliverables.

DARA: What do you mean by responsibility? What would that look like? If I'm a fly on the wall in the office where your team members are taking responsibility, what would I hear and see?

BEN: Evelyn would get the conversion report on my desk by Monday morning. Henry would be proactive about updating our slide decks with new features and communicate back to the developers what we're discovering through our market research. And Kwame would be actively looking for new market segments and setting up meetings with prospects without waiting for the latest, greatest slide deck.

DARA: What about Ramona? What would she be doing if she took responsibility for her deliverables?

BEN: Actually, she's kind of the one person on the team who already does.

DARA: OK, interesting. So let me check my understanding. What I hear you saying is that right now most of your team members are avoiding personal responsibility by complaining about each other and what you want is for them to take responsibility for their deliverables for the good of the team. Is that right?

BEN: Not quite.

DARA: What did I miss?

BEN: I think not taking responsibility for deliverables is really a function of the toxic team culture that Ramona causes. Honestly, I'd just like to get Ramona reassigned to a different team so we can get our work done.

DARA: If Ramona were off your team, what would that do for you?

BEN: Then we'd be able to express our ideas freely. Everyone would feel more ownership and take more responsibility.

DARA: And what would that allow you to accomplish?

BEN: That way, the best ideas would rise to the surface, and we'd all feel ownership of them, so we'd work hard to bring them to life.

DARA: So what I'm hearing is, what you really want is a team that generates great ideas and is committed to bringing them to life.

BEN: Yes! That's exactly what I want!

DARA: That sounds like a higher bar than just a functional team.

BEN: Yes, what I really want is a high-performing team.

DARA: Great. What does a high-performing team look like to you? You mentioned a team that generates great ideas and commits to them. Anything else?

BEN: Well, one of the reasons we don't generate great ideas is that we avoid conflict. I'd love to be on a team where we can argue over tasks and deliverables without damaging our relationships. For us to perform at that level, we need an environment where it's safe to disagree for the sake of our shared mission.

DARA: So what you want is a team where you can engage in productive conflict—disagreeing over ideas without becoming disagreeable to each other. That would allow the best ideas to get aired and implemented.

BEN: Yes, exactly!

Let's pause the dialogue here and explore that seemingly simple question—"What's the outcome you want?"—in detail.

In the following chapters, we'll revisit some of this dialogue as we look more closely at how Dara guided Ben to identify his positive, clear, and meaningful outcome.

CHAPTER 15

MAKE IT POSITIVE

TRANSFORM "DON'T WANT" INTO "DO WANT"

Often when someone complains about a situation, they haven't thought about what they would prefer instead. By focusing on what they don't want, they're distracting themselves from the possibility of imagining and going for what they do want.

This makes sense because the desire for change usually comes from frustration at a problem. And when people are frustrated by a problem, they are clear about what they *don't* want.

If they see the problem as their fault (procrastination, for example), they will often be critical of themselves ("Why can't I solve this? What's wrong with me?").

If the problem involves other people, those people are seen as obstacles, rather than resources. In Ben's mind, Ramona is the problem, which makes it most likely that he will approach her as a critic—which we've seen doesn't work.

We become allies to the people we are trying to help when we ask about the outcome—the solution—they want. This first question—*What is the outcome you want?*—shifts their focus.

Identifying the desired outcome up front also saves you a lot of time and frustration. Because you now know what you're driving toward in the conversation, you can focus on those issues and lines of inquiry relevant to that goal and ignore the red herrings. We've seen that identifying the desired outcome is like inputting a destination into a car's navigation system. Now the GPS will keep you on track and notify you and help you course-correct if you detour.

You may have to repeat the question "What is the outcome you want?" a few times, in different ways, when your conversation partner remains fixated on the problem and how bad it is or when they are gripping an intermediate goal so tightly they can't envision an end goal.

Don't:

DARA: What's the outcome you want?

BEN: I want Ramona to stop bossing people around.

DARA: OK, got it. Let's figure out how to do that.

A negative outcome like "Ramona should stop bossing people around" doesn't give Dara anything to work with. Ben is telling her what he doesn't want, rather than what he does want. A simple way to turn this around is to ask what the person would like instead.

Do:

DARA: What's the outcome you want?

BEN: I want Ramona to stop bossing people around.

DARA: What would you like instead?

BEN: Respect. Encouragement. Curiosity.

Often, one question isn't enough to turn your partner from negative to positive. You might have to ask them to flip it several times.

Do:

DARA: How would you like Ramona to interact
        with the team?

BEN: She'd stop interrupting and finding fault with our
        ideas and plans.

DARA: And if she stopped interrupting and fault-finding,
        what would she be saying and doing instead?

BEN: She'd be respectful, encouraging, and curious when
        she doesn't agree with something.

Now Ben is beginning to orient his thinking toward something he wants, rather than away from what he doesn't want. This is a much more powerful place to work from. An ideal solution can pull us toward it, enabling us to generate creative new approaches.

In *How to Have a Good Day*, Caroline Webb writes about the "Discover-Defend Axis," a feature of the human brain that approaches each situation with a fundamental question: "Is this a threat or a reward?" When we're in Defensive Mode, our brain literally loses the ability to seek out and recognize new opportunities. Instead, we focus on avoiding or mitigating bad things. In fact, Defensive Mode shifts resources into the limbic "Fight or Flight" centers of the brain and away from the frontal cortex that does planning, strategy, and other sophisticated future-oriented tasks.

Discovery Mode, on the other hand, engages parts of our brain that excel at flexibility, creativity, positivity, and exploration—exactly the qualities we need to find opportunities that take us to a better place.

What happens when our brains get stuck in Defensive Mode? We lose the ability to spot and act on opportunities.

Consider the research of Richard Wiseman, who has explored the psychological factors that lead some people to be lucky, and others not. To test his theory that lucky people create their own luck, he ran a series of experiments. In one, he first asked participants to self-identify as lucky or not, then gave them a newspaper and asked them to count the number of photographs. Unlucky people took two minutes, while lucky people managed it in seconds.

How is that possible? The "lucky" people, operating comfortably in Discovery Mode, noticed what the "unlucky" people missed: On the second page, he had printed a message that took up half the page, in two-inch-high font, that read: "Stop counting—There are 43 photographs in this newspaper."

He gave the "unlucky" folks a second chance, by placing another message in the middle of the paper. This one read: "Stop counting, tell the experimenter you have seen this and win $250." Again, they missed the opportunity because they were so focused on solving the "problem" of counting the photos.

That's why this step is so crucial in helping people change: shifting from problem orientation to outcome orientation also shifts minds from Defensive to Discovery Mode. When your conversation partner identifies their positive goal, they may spontaneously start coming up with new ideas.

Once you've gotten a positive outcome, you're ready for the next part: defining it clearly.

CHAPTER 16

MAKE IT CLEAR

GET TO SHARED CLARITY

When you first ask your partner to identify their energizing outcome, they can be pretty vague. That's especially true if this is the first time they're thinking seriously about a positive outcome. If they're using fuzzy language—big words, jargon, or generalities—ask them to define and illustrate their terms. Don't assume you know what they mean.

Or even that *they* know what they mean.

People will often have a feeling about something and use a general word to describe it, without having unpacked it themselves. Their thought, *I want a high-performing team*, might just reflect their general frustration that the team feels dysfunctional.

They may not have thought much about what a high-performing team is, what it looks like, and what it would do. And without clarity on those things, how could they hope to get there? Only when their outcome is clear will they identify the strategy and tactics to achieve it.

As their partner, *you* also need to understand what outcome they're going for. Your shared understanding will be crucial in Steps 3 and 4.

When you hear a descriptive term, recognize that you and your partner may have different ideas about what it means. It's a mistake for Dara to assume she knows what Ben means by *functional*. Ben might think that functional teams operate smoothly, without conflict. But Dara might picture spirited arguments leading to innovative new approaches. They need shared clarity to move forward together effectively.

Here's your litmus test of whether you have landed on a clear, shared vision of behavior and outcome: The outcome articulates what people are *saying* and *doing* specifically and what the *deliverables* of those behaviors look like.

Recall from the dialogue what happens when Dara stays curious and explores what Ben wants:

DARA: Tell me what a functional team would look like.
BEN: We'd stop getting in each other's way.
DARA: Tell me more. What would people be doing or saying?
BEN: Well, they'd stop complaining about each other, for one thing.
DARA: [*Noticing that Ben has gone negative again*] Great. And as a functional team, what would they do instead of complaining?
BEN: They'd take responsibility for their deliverables.
DARA: What do you mean by responsibility? What would that look like? If I'm a fly on the wall in the office where your team members are taking responsibility, what would I hear and see?
BEN: Evelyn would get the weekly scorecard on my desk by Monday morning. Henry would be proactive about alerting me to any problems that might slow down our deal flow. And Kwame would be actively looking for new market segments and setting up meetings with prospects without waiting for the latest, greatest slide deck.

DARA: What about Ramona? What would she be doing if
         she took responsibility for her deliverables?

BEN: Actually, she's kind of the one person on the team
         who already does.

The magic questions here are "What do you mean by . . . ?"
"What does that look like?" and "What would they be doing
or saying?" If you want to drive the point home hard, you can
ask, "What exactly does that look like?"

USING EMPATHY TO DRIVE CLARITY

Throughout the Outcome step, it's important and incredibly
useful to recap what you heard your partner say by sharing
your understanding and checking if it's right.

This helps you in two ways: First, you need to confirm
your understanding of their perspective in order to see what
you might be missing. Second, you build rapport when you
demonstrate your empathy. Often, you'll be the first person
who really "gets" them on this issue.

Do:

DARA: So what I hear you saying is that right now your
         team members are avoiding personal responsibil-
         ity by complaining about each other, and what you
         want is for them to take responsibility for their
         deliverables for the good of the team. Is that right?

BEN: Yes, exactly!

If they enthusiastically agree with your summary, you can
move on. If not, respond with "What did I miss?" or "What
did I get wrong?"

This last question focuses them on what they think you
didn't understand. The more effort they invest in helping you

understand their perspective to their satisfaction, the more they will value your help. You should check for understanding multiple times during the Outcome step, as this creates a strong foundation for the rest of the conversation.

Now that they've expressed the outcome in a positive and clear way, there's one more quality to go for: The outcome must be meaningful to your partner.

CHAPTER 17

MAKE IT MEANINGFUL

GET TO WHAT MATTERS

The final quality that renders an outcome energizing is that it is meaningful on its own terms. You know someone has landed on an energizing outcome when they aren't going for that outcome as a means to a greater one; this outcome *is* the greater one. It's valuable in and of itself.

Your partner's focus should be on a result that's exciting and motivating or on a new situation that is so worth achieving that they may even end up thankful for the problem that pointed to it. That's a high bar, especially if the problem is a painful one—and it's well worth going for.

Re-read this part of the dialogue to see how Dara gets Ben to identify an outcome that feels meaningful to him:

DARA: If Ramona were off your team, what would that do for you?

BEN: Then we'd be able to express our ideas freely. Everyone would feel more ownership and take more responsibility.

DARA: And what would that allow you to accomplish?

BEN: That way, the best ideas would rise to the surface, and we'd all feel ownership of them, so we'd work hard to bring them to life.

DARA: So what I'm hearing is, what you really want is a team that generates great ideas and is committed to bringing them to life.

BEN: Yes! That's exactly what I want!

DARA: That sounds like a higher bar than just a functional team.

BEN: Yes, what I really want is a high-performing team.

DARA: Great. What does a high-performing team look like to you? You mentioned a team that generates great ideas and commits to them. Anything else?

BEN: Well, one of the reasons we don't generate great ideas is that we avoid conflict. I'd love to be on a team where we can argue over tasks and deliverables without damaging our relationships. For us to perform at that level, we need an environment where it's safe to disagree for the sake of our shared mission.

Dara may have her own vision of a high-performing team. After all, lots of business books have been written on the subject, each with its own definition. Here's the thing: the "official" or "right" definition doesn't matter at all; what matters is the definition that energizes and excites Ben.

Notice how different this outcome is from the one Ben originally shared. This is why the Outcome step is so important. Had Dara simply accepted Ben's goal of removing Ramona, she would have helped him solve *that* problem and ignored this high-bar, energizing outcome.

Notice also that Dara's listening and empathy gave her an opportunity to make an observation and raise the bar on

Ben's aspiration of not just a functional team (a low bar) but a high-performing one (an energizing and higher bar).

Dara's questions move the focus from Ramona to the team's dynamics. Now there's a world of possibilities to explore; getting rid of Ramona is no longer the only solution. It's quite possible that team members intimidated into silence by Ramona will not suddenly spring into expert brainstormers and collaborators in her absence. Rather than being the cause of the dysfunction, Ramona's behavior might be more of a symptom.

So when someone identifies an outcome that is simply the opposite of their problem (e.g. remove Ramona from the team), that's a signal for you to probe further. In the following dialogue, Ginger thinks she has a motivation problem.

Don't:

GINGER: I'm doing really well on my new exercise program, but I'm scared because I've done this before, and then it just falls by the wayside. I'd really like help maintaining my enthusiasm about it.

FRED: Great, let's work on ways to keep up that enthusiasm! What do you like best about exercising?

Do:

GINGER: I'm doing really well on my new exercise program, but I'm scared because I've done this before, and then it just falls by the wayside. I'd really like help maintaining my enthusiasm about it.

FRED: If you were to maintain your enthusiasm, what would that allow you to accomplish?

GINGER: Well, I'd exercise every day and wouldn't give up when I don't feel like it.

FRED: OK, so is it fair to say that what you really want is to exercise every day? No matter whether you feel like it or not? Even when you're not enthusiastic about it?

The problem with solving for enthusiasm—or any feeling or attitude—is that we can't really control how we feel about something. Ginger is expressing an unconscious rule here, one that Fred has to deconstruct in order to help Ginger change.

The rule is "In order to exercise, I must be enthusiastic about exercise." And chances are, that unspoken rule has been the problem in the past; when Ginger wakes up and "doesn't feel like it," she concludes that she just isn't going to get on her stationary bicycle. Fred can help Ginger become a daily exerciser by offering her the chance to drop that belief and replace it with an empowering one: "I exercise every day because I want to be fit and healthy as I age; it doesn't matter whether I feel like it on any particular day."

When you hear an outcome that doesn't seem like the thing they really want, dig a little. You can phrase it like Fred did, earlier: "What would that allow you to do?" One of my favorite questions to get to a deeper level of meaning is simply, "For the sake of what?"

At this point, you will have a positive, clear, and meaningful agreed-upon picture of their energizing outcome. Now you can move to Step 3: finding an opportunity in the problem to bring about that outcome.

STEP 3

FIND THE HIDDEN OPPORTUNITY

CHAPTER 18

Become a Scientist

They're Not Learning from You; They're Learning with You

Carl Reiner and Mel Brooks's *2000 Year Old Man* tells the story of how humans discovered God. First, they worshipped the leader of their tribe, a cruel and powerful man named Phil. "One day, Phil was hit by lightning. And we looked up, we said, 'There's something bigger than Phil!'"

There's something bigger than your partner's problem. In Step 3, you're going to find out what.

Ben started out by complaining about Ramona. In his mind, she was the problem. By asking about Ben's energizing outcome, Dara helped him identify what he really wants: a high-performing team.

Now Dara will help Ben see Ramona's behavior, not simply as an obstacle, but as an opportunity to help him achieve the outcome he wants.

When you're at Step 3 with your partner, you want to get them to a point where they can honestly say, "Thank goodness for this problem! I thought it was a brick wall, but it turned out to be a door."

So how do we get there?

First, circle back to the problem. Explore what's happening now and what your partner has already tried in their attempts to solve it. You have a couple of goals here. You want to continue to build empathy and connection, and you want to dig beneath their stories and interpretations to get to the data: the facts and details.

Then you'll search for hidden opportunities. You'll explore the potential upsides to the problem—how it might be positive, useful, or valuable. And you'll explore the gap between the energizing outcome and what's happening now, identifying what's missing or what's in the way. What you're looking for is how the thing they thought was a problem turns out to be a key part of the solution.

Because this is a counterintuitive process, you run the risk of generating resistance if you bulldoze your way from problem to opportunity. You want to give your partner ample time to talk about the problem and take your time in making sure you understand their experience and perspective to their satisfaction. You will be most successful if you approach this part of the conversation with curiosity.

In his book *Sapiens*, Juval Noah Harari identifies one of the key qualities of the Scientific Revolution as "the willingness to admit ignorance." He writes, "The Scientific Revolution has not been a revolution of knowledge. It has been, above all, a revolution of ignorance. The great discovery that launched the Scientific Revolution was the discovery that humans do not know the answers to their most important questions."

The most helpful mindset you can adopt in this part of the process is a willingness to "not know," to recognize that any knee-jerk solutions are premature. This can be very challenging because we don't like not knowing. It's not fun. It doesn't make us feel good or competent or even helpful. (For more on the power of not knowing, check out my TEDx talk, "I Don't Know," at BregmanPartners.com/change.)

If you're a leader or manager (or parent or, frankly, almost anyone), you may hang your identity on having answers. "If I don't know," you might be thinking deep down, "Then what use am I?"

The answer is: of tremendous use. At this stage, not knowing is precisely how you will be most helpful.

Because not knowing leaves room for learning.

And you don't need to know because—and this is really important:

They're not learning *from* you; they're learning *with* you.

You are an effective thinking partner because you're discovering together. You're not a teacher, talking down to your student, imparting your great wisdom. You're not asking rhetorical or leading questions that make the other person feel like a kid at school trying to figure out the "right" answer the teacher is waiting for.

You're an ally. You're tackling this together.

THE OPPORTUNITY STEP IN ACTION

The Opportunity step is built around three lines of inquiry:

1. What's happening now? (Take a detailed look at the problem.)
2. What have you tried? (Create a comprehensive list of attempted solutions.)
3. How can you use the problem to achieve your energizing outcome? (Find the opportunity afforded by the problem.)

Let's see how Dara takes Ben through the Opportunity step, finding his path to a high-performing team. As a reminder, we paused the dialogue here:

DARA: Great. What does a high-performing team look like
        to you? You mentioned a team that generates great
        ideas and commits to them. Anything else?

BEN: Well, one of the reasons we don't generate great
        ideas is that we avoid conflict. I'd love to be on a
        team where we can argue over tasks and deliverables
        without damaging our relationships. For us to
        perform at that level, we need an environment
        where it's safe to disagree for the sake of our
        shared mission.

Now Dara and Ben explore how Ramona's behavior can
contribute to Ben's outcome of a high-performing team.

WHAT'S HAPPENING NOW?

DARA: Got it. Tell me what's happening now.

BEN: Ramona isn't the leader, but she acts like she is—
        and not a very good one. She keeps bossing every-
        one around.

DARA: Can you give me a specific example?

BEN: Sure, at yesterday's meeting she was at it again.

DARA: Can you take me there? If I were a fly on the wall,
        what would I see and hear?

BEN: I was presenting a slide with the results of ad testing,
        and she interrupted me with, "Your data isn't reli-
        able." Then she went off on a rant about how we're
        writing ad copy without having done in-depth
        customer avatar analysis.

DARA: Tell me more.

BEN: She said that because we don't know enough about
        our ideal customer psychographics, we can't write
        compelling ads. Therefore, the response rates are

meaningless. Which means we're making product decisions based on a market segment that will never be our customer.

DARA: Then what happened?

BEN: I told her that I got the data from analytics, and they'd verified it. And that she could please wait her turn and ask questions when I was done.

DARA: What did she do or say in response to that?

BEN: She huffed and was quiet for the rest of the meeting. Now she's avoiding me, and ignoring my emails, in a really passive-aggressive way.

WHAT HAVE YOU TRIED?

DARA: What specifically have you tried in the past to deal with this dynamic with Ramona?

BEN: I've tried talking over her when she interrupts.

DARA: How did that go?

BEN: Not well. She got louder and more aggressive.

DARA: What else?

BEN: I asked her to stop interrupting and wait her turn. I was actually kind of mad and, I admit, I was a little aggressive about it.

DARA: And what happened then?

BEN: She withdrew from the conversation and didn't participate for the rest of the meeting. She just sat there stewing.

DARA: How did you respond to that?

BEN: I just continued on, but I felt bad—like I had done something wrong. It was really uncomfortable.

DARA: What did the rest of the team do then?

BEN: Stony silence. Come to think of it, they had been pretty quiet before then too. Not much discussion

or interaction, just listening to one presentation
after another.

DARA: What else have you tried?

BEN: Well, I used to double-check the data obsessively for
a couple of days before each meeting.

DARA: Did that help?

BEN: Not really. It annoyed me and wasted my time.

DARA: And what else have you tried?

BEN: Once I emailed Ramona before the meeting and
asked her to help me create the slide. We worked
together for an hour, and the meeting went great.

DARA: That's interesting. What did that look like when
you were collaborating? Can you let me be a fly
on the wall?

BEN: She came to my office and I asked her what were
the most important points I needed to get onto
the slide.

DARA: And then?

BEN: She showed me a flow chart she'd created with a
bunch of go/no-go gates and asked what metrics I'd
want to see at each gate to justify the next investment of time and money.

DARA: Was that helpful?

BEN: Actually, it was. Very.

DARA: And what else have you tried?

BEN: That's pretty much it.

HOW CAN YOU USE THE PROBLEM TO ACHIEVE YOUR ENERGIZING OUTCOME?

DARA: OK. We've talked about how Ramona gets in the
way, how her behavior is problematic, and that you
get frustrated and annoyed by it. I hear that clearly.

And it also sounds like there are ways in which she has been helpful. Now I want to ask you a different question, and I'd like you to take a few moments to think before you answer. Ready?

BEN: Yeah?

DARA: What's good about Ramona's bad behavior? I know it's annoying and can feel disrespectful. Without minimizing that, is there anything productive, positive, useful, or of value that it brings to the team?

BEN: [*Long pause*]

DARA: [*Silently waiting*]

BEN: Well, I guess what's also true is that she's willing to say things that other people aren't. To raise the undiscussables.

DARA: That sounds like boldness.

BEN: Yeah, and I guess it's also a willingness to risk friendly relationships for the sake of what we're trying to accomplish.

DARA: Can you give me an example of how she does it?

BEN: Actually, yes. Everybody sort of knows that the data's sketchy, but Ramona was the only person to really say it out loud. Nobody else spoke up. Which I get—acknowledging it would set us back at least a month. We'd have to start again from scratch and find a better market research firm. Ramona spoke up when the rest of us sort of just looked the other way.

DARA: That's a great example. Sounds like Ramona is playing an uncomfortable but important role. And that the silence of the rest of the team—while easier to overlook because it's polite and quiet and comfortable—is actually also an obstacle to the team being a high-performing team.

BEN: Yeah, the rest of the team—and I include myself here—actually prefer to be nice and polite to each other, rather than raise difficult issues.

DARA: How does that get in the way of what you're trying to accomplish?

BEN: Well, it seriously undermines risk management. We can't prepare for what we aren't willing to acknowledge and discuss.

DARA: Anything else?

BEN: I think we're missing the best ideas. The first one that someone comes up with gets adopted because, you know, it's pretty good and we just compliment them. Asking for other ideas seems like it would be rude.

DARA: Got it. So I'm hearing that, even leaving the issue of Ramona out of it for the moment, there are other things getting in the way of you having a high-performing team. Does that sound right?

BEN: Yes, absolutely.

DARA: Can you list them?

BEN: Well, like I said, we prefer politeness to honesty. We aren't willing to engage in conflict for the sake of better thinking or risk mitigation.

DARA: Anything else?

BEN: That's the crux of it.

DARA: Here's what I'm hearing then: Even though her aggressive approach blocks other people's good ideas, removing Ramona from the team isn't a great path to high performance because no one would be willing to speak up and challenge groupthink. Am I thinking about this right?

BEN: Yes. Removing her might make it worse. She brings a quality of gutsiness that our team—again, me included—really needs.

DARA: That's so interesting. Given that, what would your high-performing team look and sound like?

BEN: We'd be as sensitive as I am and as brave as Ramona.

DARA: As sensitive as you and as brave as Ramona. That's compelling. And I can feel your excitement. Sensitive and brave at the same time?

BEN: More or less. If Ramona could just learn to speak her mind without alienating the rest of us, and the rest of us could learn to speak honestly and raise important issues, then we'd really get somewhere.

DARA: So while Ramona's the problem . . .

BEN: She holds a key piece of the solution.

DARA: So can I rephrase what we're going for here?

BEN: Yes, please.

DARA: In order to achieve a high-performing team, you want to create a culture where everyone speaks their truth with care and sensitivity, and commits to speaking, listening, and being open to hard truths for the sake of the team, the best outcomes, and their own growth and development. Did I get that right?

BEN: Yes, totally. Now I'm actually kind of excited about building that high-performing team, because I see that I've got all the pieces already. And yes, Ramona is part of the problem, but not the whole problem. I'm part of the problem too—as are the others on the team. And, together, we're the solution. I just have to figure out how to integrate those pieces.

DARA: That does sound exciting!

BEN: It's like we have two completely different cultures
        on the team—ours and Ramona's. Neither is right
        or wrong. Both are necessary for high performance.
        So how do I merge them?

Let's stop here. In the next few chapters, we'll revisit parts
of this dialogue to unpack and explore how Dara used the
three questions to help Ben discover his hidden opportunity.

CHAPTER 19

QUESTION 1: WHAT'S HAPPENING NOW?

EXPLORE THE PROBLEM IN DEPTH

Why, you might be wondering, do we wait until Step 3 to explore the problem in depth?

Because before now, the answer would have been haphazard, rambling, and misleading.

Here's why: Before, when your partner was focused on the problem, they would have described what's happening *in relation to the problem* they thought they had.

Now though? We can guide them to describe what's happening *in relation to the outcome* they want. That could not happen before clarifying the outcome.

Your goal is to collect data (the facts of the situation), as well as get your partner's perspective on that data. Essentially, you want to see what they see and how they see it. This will give you the basic shape of the situation, help you empathize with their point of view, and begin to explore where and how their interpretation of that situation is getting in the way of the outcome they want.

A reminder I can't share often enough: Keep your empathy level high here (without taking on their emotions as your own).

When people describe their unsatisfactory situations, they can get down on themselves. Sometimes they express this as self-criticism, and sometimes they project it outward, blaming others for the situation. The more you build rapport—understanding without judging and being the ally who believes in their capabilities and positive intentions—the less defensive they will become. This is important because, as we've seen, defensiveness blocks creativity, and without creativity, they will just keep repeating the same ineffective strategies.

It's crucial that you remain genuinely curious so that you don't just follow this process as a checklist. If you're actually curious—curious like a wide-eyed 6-year-old to whom the world is still wonderful and fascinating—this process will feel natural to you and your partner. If you're trying to "fake" curiosity, your partner will sense that you don't really care.

Don't:

DARA: Tell me what's happening now with your team.
BEN: Ramona isn't the leader, but she keeps bossing everyone around.
DARA: Uh-huh. So what have you tried?

In this dialogue, Dara isn't curious about what's actually happening. Instead, she's accepted the label that Ben slapped on the situation: "Ramona is bossing everyone around." In other words, Ramona herself is the problem. If that's true, then the only solutions are to get rid of Ramona or neutralize her influence in some other way.

Don't accept your partner's labels. Instead, ask them to describe specifically what's going on.

Do:

DARA: Tell me what's happening now with your team.
BEN: Ramona isn't the leader, but she keeps bossing everyone around.

DARA: Tell me more about that. What exactly is she doing and saying?

BEN: She talks over people in meetings and argues with everyone about features and priorities. She's convinced that she has the answer and the rest of us are idiots.

Dara asks for hard facts, rather than labels or interpretations of those facts, in three ways.

First, she asks Ben, "Tell me more." Second, she deliberately uses the word *exactly*. Third, she asks for behaviors, what Ramona is "doing and saying."

In response, Ben shares specific facts: talking over people and focusing on features and priorities. He also offers interpretations which Dara will explore further: Ramona is arguing, and she does so because she feels superior.

Dara's most important job here is to stay in empathy, while neither accepting nor debating Ben's interpretations. One of the great gifts you can give your partner is the flexibility to consider possibilities other than the one they've landed on. It's not easy; our brains are meaning-making machines, and even when we don't know the reason for something, we're more than happy to fill in the gaps without even realizing it. Don't buy into their interpretation.

Don't:

BEN: She argues with everyone. She's convinced that she has the answer and the rest of us are idiots.

DARA: That's a big problem.

And don't get into a debate either.

Don't:

BEN: She argues with everyone. She's convinced that she has the answer and the rest of us are idiots.

DARA: Maybe she's arguing because she wants the project
         to succeed and she thinks you guys are all missing
         something important.

Instead, affirm that they may be right, and gently push
them to consider other alternatives.

Do:

BEN: She argues with everyone. She's convinced that she
         has the answer and the rest of us are idiots.
DARA: That's definitely one explanation. And I'm won-
         dering what else might be true? Are there other
         possibilities you can think of for Ramona's ten-
         dency to argue?
BEN: I suppose she might be frustrated that no one else is
         raising these objections. She might not even believe
         them herself, I guess. She could be just trying to lay
         all the risk out on the table for our consideration.

When someone is stuck in a problem, they will always
have a narrative about it. Sometimes they construct their
narrative—consciously or unconsciously—to protect them
from having to change.

For example, Ramona may argue because she thinks everyone else is an idiot, not because she sees something that her team
is missing. If I don't get a promotion, I may think it's because
my boss hates me, not because the person who was chosen
instead had skills and experiences deemed more suitable.

People stuck in a problem need your help to move beyond
that narrative.

By asking what else might be going on, you can help your
partner see that their narrative isn't the only—or even the
most likely—one. And that realization can cool their anger or
resentment, which creates space for creativity and outcome-
focused brainstorming.

SEPARATING DATA FROM INTERPRETATION

Here's a principle that applies throughout all the steps and is of utmost importance here: Dig past the generalizations, characterizations, and unclear language to get to the specifics of what's actually happening in the situation. Not what *always* happens or what *usually* happens. But what *has* happened. What people are saying and doing. Specifically.

Like we saw in the Outcome step, specificity will help you expose blind spots to see what the other person doesn't yet see—a critical move to help them unearth an opportunity they don't yet realize is there.

But one thing that makes this different from the Outcome step is that now the person is not *imagining* a future they want to create; they're *describing* a past that has already occurred.

That changes our technique. We can have our partner bring us to real examples—specific times and places where they've seen something. We're collecting data like a scientist.

Begin by asking about what's happening now. You'll get a general idea of the problem—its nature, scope, and intensity. That's all helpful—but not sufficient. Once you understand enough to probe for details and patterns, start asking for specific stories and examples.

Our conversation partners will almost always default to generalizations when we ask about their persistent and sticky problems and challenges. So what's the point of diving deeper to get more specific information?

Because generalizations are part of the reason they're stuck.

Any generalization, by definition, must focus on certain aspects of a situation while ignoring or minimizing others. Generalizations, by their very nature, include blind spots. They "lock in" one interpretation in particular: the interpretation that's keeping your conversation partner stuck. Helping them create a different story will open their mind to new ways of approaching the issue.

You're looking to elicit details that are relevant, but which your conversation partner omitted from their narrative.

One way our partner can get stuck is to create a story about what "always" or "usually" happens. When our partners speak in generalities, they're unconsciously constructing that story. It's their narrative.

What makes that kind of default narrative possible is oversimplification: seeing the situation as black and white, right and wrong, good and bad.

We need to add a little complexity to their simple narrative. When they simplify by generalizing, they leave out details that may be significant. They gloss over specific words and actions.

So when you hear a generalization, it's a signal that this might be a good place to dig deeper.

While you're getting your partner's story about what happened, you want to probe for what they don't see and what they perceive in a biased fashion that's getting in the way of creative new approaches. Asking someone to tell you about a moment, in detail, can bring to light things they gloss over, miss, misinterpret, and deny.

Remember that our partner has probably rehashed this problem in their mind dozens or hundreds of times already. If they could solve their problem based on what they think they know, they already would have.

Even though you don't necessarily know what you're digging for, dig anyway. Typically, you won't recognize the significance of any of these facts until later in the process. Think of a suspenseful movie or novel; you'll read details in the early chapters that don't seem like a big deal, but later become pivotal to the plot. It's these details that will allow both of you to reframe the problem into an opportunity.

Speaking of suspenseful dramas, here's a metaphor to help you think about the value of specifics. You know that scene in the crime drama where the main character, some kind of detective, asks to see the security footage that so far has yielded no clues to the other investigators? First, the detective watches the video at full speed. That's the "tell me more" and "go on" part. They're getting the general outline: the scene, the time, the broad unfolding of events.

Then they watch it again, slower. They instruct the video technician: "Rewind 10 seconds. Play. Rewind again. Freeze frame . . . now. Zoom. Top left corner. More . . . more . . . There! Do you see it?" And there's the reflection of the killer's license plate in the sideview mirror of the truck parked across the street or the image of a watch face proving that the video time stamp was incorrect and therefore the perp's alibi doesn't hold water.

You slo-mo, freeze, and zoom the scene with the specificity prompts:

- What does/did that look like?
- Take me there.
- Let me be a fly on the wall.
- What did you/they do and say, specifically?

You want to get to the point where the person is describing what people are saying and doing. Since you're not actually watching the movie, you have to imagine it as they speak. If you can't picture something, ask about it.

HOW TO SHIFT FROM GENERALIZATIONS TO SPECIFICS

First, get in the habit of recognizing the clues that your partner is talking in generalizations. Let the words *always*, *generally*, *typically*, *usually*, and all verbs in the present tense become little alarm bells that you need to ask for a specific example, and then ask them to describe what they're seeing and hearing.

Do:

BEN: She argues with everyone. She's convinced that she has the answer and the rest of us are idiots.

DARA: Can you give me a specific example?

BEN: Sure, at yesterday's meeting she was at it again.

DARA: Take me there. What did she say and do?

BEN: I was presenting a slide with the results of ad testing, and she interrupted me with, "I don't think this data is reliable."

Now Dara has some facts to work with: Ben was presenting, and Ramona said, "I don't think this data is reliable."

Once your partner is telling an actual story in the form of "This happened, then that, then that, then that," you want to encourage them to keep going. To tell more of the story. To fill in more details.

There are two simple ways to get them to keep going. If they're telling a story and you want to know what happens next, sequentially, ask, "Then what happened?"

If you want more detail about something they've already described, then say, "Tell me more." Both demonstrate your interest, and both are open-ended, allowing your partner the freedom to share details you might never think to ask about.

Don't:

BEN: I was presenting a slide with the results of ad testing, and she interrupted me with, "I don't think this data is reliable."

DARA: Did you tell her to wait her turn?

Do:

BEN: I was presenting a slide with the results of ad testing, and she interrupted me with, "I don't think this data is reliable."

DARA: Then what happened?

BEN: I told her that I got the data from analytics, and they'd verified it. And that she could please wait her turn and ask questions when I was done.

Do:

BEN: Ramona went off on a rant about how we're writing ad copy without having done in-depth customer avatar analysis.

DARA: Tell me more.

BEN: She said that because we don't know enough about our ideal customer psychographics, we can't write compelling ads. Therefore, the data we get from them is useless.

Another way to get more information about what they've told you is to repeat the last word or phrase as a question.

Do:

BEN: I've talked to Henry, but he's unwilling to do anything.

DARA: Unwilling to do anything?

BEN: He said that since we'll be handing the campaign off to a marketing agency in a couple of months, it's not worth rocking the boat right now.

Drilling down to the specifics can feel a little interrogative. You're pushing them to go beyond their narrative. You may even interrupt them at times to keep them focused and going deeper. That can be uncomfortable. Keep expressing empathy to help them be more open to seeing things they may not have been able or willing to see before.

Once you have a clear and specific picture of what happened, you can move to the next inquiry: what your partner has already tried.

CHAPTER 20

QUESTION 2: WHAT HAVE YOU TRIED?

WHAT WORKED AND WHAT DIDN'T?

Once you have explored the problem, the next task is to find out what your partner has tried in order to solve the problem.

This serves two purposes. First, it helps them observe their past behavior more objectively. If tactics didn't work, they should see that clearly. Steven C. Hayes, founder of ACT (Acceptance and Commitment Training), calls this process "creative hopelessness." Only when they can clearly see they're banging their head against a wall—that their current strategy is hopeless—will they be open to creative new alternatives.

Second, it helps your partner uncover strategies that worked in the past, either partially or fully, that they can resurrect, intensify, adapt, or combine. "Oh, yeah," they'll say, smacking their forehead. "When I used to journal in the morning, I was able to control my sweet tooth throughout the day. Thanks!"

The technique here is simple. Ask some version of "What have you tried to solve/deal with/address this issue/problem/situation?"

Avoid the temptation to prejudge the results of those efforts.

Don't:

DARA: Tell me about the times you were unsuccessful in dealing with Ramona.

BEN: How much time do you have?

Do:

DARA: What have you tried in the past to deal with this dynamic with Ramona?

BEN: I've tried talking over her when she interrupts.

DARA: Think of a specific time when you did that. What happened?

BEN: I talked over her and she just got louder and more aggressive. I backed down.

AND WHAT ELSE?

You want to generate an exhaustive list of past strategies so your partner can figure out what might work now and what probably won't. Going through that list will also help your partner appreciate the value of coming up with new solutions.

How will you know if a past strategy was effective? Ask them. And keep it open-ended; a closed-ended question will elicit a "Yes" or "No," which tells you very little.

Don't:

DARA: What else have you tried?

BEN: Well, I used to double-check the data obsessively for a couple of days before each meeting.

DARA: Did that help?

BEN: Nope.

Instead, ask a question that requires a more thoughtful answer.

Do:

BEN: Well, I used to double-check the data obsessively for a couple of days before each meeting.

DARA: And what happened?

Keep your question neutral. Don't judge what they've done or predict the outcome. Remain curious, almost innocent like a child.

Don't:

BEN: Well, I used to double-check the data obsessively for a couple of days before each meeting.

DARA: I bet that got you nowhere.

AND WHAT ELSE?

Keep going as long as your partner comes up with new strategies. And here's a nuance that's worth mentioning: "And what else?" is more effective than "Anything else?" because the latter is a closed-ended question that's easy to answer with a "No."

Don't:

DARA: OK. Anything else?

BEN: Nope, that's about it.

Do:

DARA: OK. And what else?

BEN: Last year, I asked HR to recommend a sensitivity training she could take.

Keep going with "and what else" until they tell you that they're done.

DARA: And what else have you tried?

BEN: That's all I can think of.

WHAT DID THAT LOOK LIKE?

When your partner mentions a strategy that has worked, at least somewhat, you should explore that strategy in more depth and with specificity, using the "fly on the wall" technique.

DARA: And what else have you tried?
BEN: Once I emailed Ramona before the meeting and asked her to help me create the slide. We worked together for an hour, and the meeting went great.
DARA: Wow, that's interesting. What did that look like when you were collaborating? Can you let me be a fly on the wall?
BEN: She came to my office and I asked her what were the most important points I needed to get onto the slide.

Again, you can use any of the specificity-generating prompts we've already seen:

"What did that look like?"

"Take me there when you tried that."

"What happened when you tried that? Let me be a fly on the wall."

Resist the urge to point out what may seem obvious to you: that they already have a solution that they're just not using.

Don't:
DARA: Sounds like you just solved your own problem. Next time, why don't you just invite Ramona to collaborate with you again?

BEN: Yeah, I could do that. [*Thinking, "I'd rather have a root canal without anesthesia than spend an hour pretending to value her opinion."*]

Instead, keep asking about what happened. Go back to the "What's happening now?" questions to get a detailed picture of this prior success (whether full or partial, it doesn't really matter). Your goal is to let your partners hear themselves describe effective approaches, rather than waiting for you to prescribe them. They'll accumulate a list that we will draw from soon enough. In the meantime, help them uncover particular elements to the approach that helped them to be successful.

Do:

BEN: Ramona came to my office and I asked her what were the most important points I needed to get onto the slide.

DARA: And then?

BEN: She showed me a flow chart she'd created with a bunch of go/no-go gates and asked my opinion about what metrics I'd want to see at each gate to justify the next investment of time and money.

PAST ATTEMPTS CAN TELL YOU WHY THEY'RE STUCK

When someone tells you about the things that they've already tried to solve a problem that have been unsuccessful, listen for clues that they're trying to solve the wrong problem.

A manufacturing client of mine had spent years trying to improve the quality of their shipped products, without success. Going through the "What have you tried?" part of the conversation, I saw that they knew exactly how to solve quality problems and had deployed various approaches and best practices without achieving lasting results.

They knew *how* to solve their quality problem; they just weren't following through on what they knew they needed to do. It would have taken time and money and delayed shipments to clients. Their quality problem was sticky because they weren't willing to trade current and future revenue for a serious commitment to quality.

In other words, they didn't have a *quality* problem; they had a *commitment* problem.

Once that became apparent, we shifted our focus to building a company-wide commitment to endure the short-term pain of missing deadlines and potential revenue (along with the heat from Wall Street, unhappy clients, and diminished bonuses). With this in place, they turned their quality problem around in a single quarter. (See one of the sample dialogues at BregmanPartners.com/change for a fictionalized conversation inspired by this client.)

WHAT IF THEY HAVEN'T TRIED ANYTHING?

Sometimes your partner hasn't yet attempted to solve the problem due to a prolonged case of analysis-paralysis. When you hear that, don't despair. You now have a clear direction to move them in: taking some action for the purpose of learning.

When someone gets their car stuck in mud, it's very common to watch them spin their wheels faster and faster in an attempt to escape from the trap. And if you've ever watched this (from a safe place, ideally not directly behind the spinning wheel), you know how counterproductive that is: the more the wheel spins, the deeper it gets stuck.

Your partner can do the same thing with their mental wheels, analyzing and reanalyzing the past, and getting more and more convinced that there's nothing to be done. The cure here is to shake up their perception by getting them to try something they haven't tried before. Even if it doesn't work, it will provide some feedback that can spur more creative thinking.

CHAPTER 21

QUESTION 3: HOW CAN YOU USE THE PROBLEM TO ACHIEVE YOUR ENERGIZING OUTCOME?

THANK GOODNESS FOR THIS PROBLEM

At this point, you and your conversation partner should have a clear sense of the outcome they want, a detailed picture of what's happening now, as well as a catalog of what they've tried in the past.

You've built rapport, decoupled the data from their interpretation of that data, and highlighted the gap between what is and what they want. Essentially, you've been laying out the facts in relation to their energizing outcome.

That's no small thing. Often, just asking people about what they really want, and what people are actually doing and saying (rather than accepting labels such as *obnoxious* or *dysfunctional*), can give rise to a fresh perspective and open new possibilities for action.

That sets us up for the next phase of the Opportunity step, in which you guide them to use the problem to help achieve the energizing outcome. What you're looking for is the opportunity hiding in the problem. Where there's a problem, there's an opportunity, as illustrated by the saying, "Never let a good crisis go to waste."

In many stellar organizations, for example, problems are celebrated as doorways to systemic improvements. When a line worker pulls the kill switch to stop production because of a defective part, everyone cheers. Because they now have a chance to fix, not just the defective part, but the processes that created it so it won't happen again.

Help your partner discover the opportunity by asking variations of a simple and powerful question: "How can you use this problem to get what you want?" In other words, you want to get them to a place where they can sincerely say, "Thank goodness I had this problem."

It takes some faith (and possibly emotional courage) to dive in here, because you don't know exactly what you're looking for. But I assure you, there's something there. There are as many different hidden opportunities as there are situations and no way to predict the opportunity in a given situation.

Fortunately, there are several common categories into which most opportunities fall. In this chapter, I'll show you how to recognize those categories and develop the opportunities they present. In any particular conversation, you may find opportunities that fit into more than one category.

We'll take our time in this chapter to go deep—I'll offer a number of different tactics to help you navigate this challenging and transformative step.

FIND THE UPSIDE IN THE DOWNSIDE

Almost always, a problem is two-sided. It has a conspicuous downside and a cloaked upside.

One common category of opportunity involves finding a positive aspect of the problem. You can probe for the "upside of the downside" by asking questions like these: "Is there anything good about this problem?" or "Is there a way to exploit the problem to achieve the energizing outcome?"

For example, Ramona is aggressive (downside) and because of that—not despite it—she can help move her team forward on important issues (upside).

Be curious and humble. Offer observations and float theories for your partner's consideration. Here, Dara patiently guides Ben to the opportunity of a high-performing team. Don't underestimate the importance of the long pause. Dara's willingness to wait—to give Ben space to process the question and give a brave and vulnerable answer—is crucial to unlocking the opportunity.

Do:

DARA: OK. We've talked about how Ramona gets in the way, how her behavior is problematic, and that you get frustrated and annoyed by it. I hear that clearly. Now, I want to ask you a different question, and I'd like you to take a few moments to think before you answer. Ready?

BEN: Yeah?

DARA: What's good about Ramona's bad behavior? Without minimizing how annoying and frustrating it feels, is there anything productive, positive, useful, or of value that it brings to the team?

BEN: [*Long pause*]

DARA: [*Silently waiting*]

BEN: Well, I guess what's also true is that she's willing to say things that other people aren't. To raise the undiscussables.

Ben's answer to the question, "Is there anything productive, positive, useful, or of value that Ramona's behavior brings to the team?"—her willingness to raise the undiscussables—highlights a new obstacle to Ben's energizing outcome of a high-performing team: their collective reluctance to raise difficult issues.

Next, Dara will help Ben get there, not just by asking questions, but by sharing an observation—"that sounds like boldness"—to which Ben could respond.

DARA: That sounds like boldness.

BEN: Yeah, and I guess it's also a willingness to risk friendly relationships for the sake of what we're trying to accomplish. The rest of the team—and I include myself here—actually prefer to be nice and polite to each other, rather than raise difficult issues.

DARA: How does that get in the way of what you're trying to accomplish?

BEN: Well, it seriously undermines risk management. We can't prepare for what we aren't willing to acknowledge and discuss.

DARA: Anything else?

BEN: I think we're missing the best ideas. The first one that someone comes up with gets adopted because, you know, it's pretty good and we just compliment them. Asking for other ideas seems like it would be rude.

Dara then guides Ben to identify all additional obstacles to his energizing outcome.

DARA: So I'm hearing that, even leaving the issue of Ramona out of it for the moment, there are other things getting in the way of you having a high-performing team. Does that sound right?

BEN: Yes, absolutely.

DARA: Can you list them?

BEN: Well, like I said, we prefer politeness to honesty. We aren't willing to engage in conflict for the sake of better thinking or risk mitigation.

DARA: Anything else?

BEN: That's the crux of it.

DARA: Here's what I'm hearing then: Even though her
           aggressive approach blocks other people's good
           ideas, removing Ramona from the team isn't
           a great path to high performance because no
           one would be willing to speak up and challenge
           groupthink. Am I thinking about this right?

BEN: Yes. Removing her might make it worse. While
           the analytical/intuitive dynamic is real, I think the
           main thing is, she brings a quality of gutsiness that
           our team—again, me included—really needs.

Juxtaposing the original problem—Ramona's aggressiveness—
with the larger, previously unacknowledged and unaddressed
problem—the team's diffidence—highlights an opportunity:
Ramona can learn from her teammates to speak with sensitivity, and they can learn from her to practice a more radical form
of honesty.

As you guide your conversation partner to explore the
upside of the problem, take care not to dismiss it or minimize
its impact. If you argue, "Hey, this is really a great opportunity
in disguise," you'll lose rapport.

Don't:

DARA: You keep complaining about Ramona, but you're
           ignoring all her positive qualities. Tell me about
           what's good about having Ramona on your team.

BEN: [*Thinking, "You've got to be kidding."*] It's always so
           nice and stress-free when she's on vacation.

Sometimes it takes multiple offers to get your partner to
go there. Don't force it. Instead, approach the question from
other angles. If their problem is with another person, guide

them to empathize with that person. One way is to ask about that person's positive intentions.

Do:

DARA: What's good about Ramona's bad behavior? I know it's annoying and can feel disrespectful. Without minimizing that, is there anything productive, positive, useful, or of value that it brings to the team?

BEN: No. She's poison.

DARA: If you asked Ramona what she's trying to accomplish by speaking up so aggressively in meetings, what do you think she'd say?

BEN: [*Long pause*]

DARA: [*Silently waiting*]

BEN: Probably that she's trying to wake us up to risks we haven't considered.

Or you can ask what a positive and useful purpose *might* be.

Do:

BEN: No. She's poison.

DARA: I hear you. And when you look at Ramona's behavior, what's the absolute most positive spin you can put on it? If her motives were totally selfless, and she really cared about the team, what might she be trying to accomplish, however clumsily and annoyingly?

BEN: Well, I guess you could say that she doesn't want to get blindsided by unseen risk.

After identifying the upside to Ramona's behavior as boldness, Dara next asks for a specific example—back to the "fly on the wall" technique you learned in the Outcome step.

This allows them to get shared clarity on the concept of "boldness" and makes it real for Ben.

DARA: Can you give me an example?
BEN: Actually, yes. Everybody sort of knows that the
           data's sketchy, but Ramona was the only person
           to really say it out loud. Nobody else spoke up.
           Which I get. It's scary because acknowledging it
           would set us back by at least a month. We'd have
           to start again from scratch and find a better mar-
           ket research firm. Ramona spoke up when the rest
           of us sort of just looked the other way.

Ben acknowledges that even if Ramona quit tomorrow, he would still be leading a team of people who prioritize nice- ness over performance and who don't have the capacity to engage in fruitful conflict.

Here's where you invite your partner to reexamine their assumption that the presenting problem was the only thing keeping them from their goal:

DARA: Here's what I'm hearing then: Even though her
           aggressive approach blocks other people's good
           ideas, removing Ramona from the team isn't
           a great path to high performance because no
           one would be willing to speak up and challenge
           groupthink. Am I thinking about this right?
BEN: Yes. Removing her might make it worse. She
           brings a quality of gutsiness that our team—again,
           me included—really needs.

By now, Ben has realized that Ramona's behavior isn't the only obstacle to a high-performing team. The timid team culture also gets in the way. And Ramona can be the solution.

Unfortunately, we often ignore, miss, or deny the upside, because the downside is so glaring and painful. We don't see Ramona's potential for a positive impact because her aggressiveness is so off-putting. The opportunity here is to recognize that the upside everyone is missing can have a meaningful and positive impact on a situation.

FIND THE SYSTEM UPGRADE OPPORTUNITY

System upgrade opportunities exist when an individual problem can shed light on a potential improvement to the larger organization or system. You can uncover these opportunities by asking, "How can we solve this problem in a way that improves the larger system?"

Consider an engineering start-up with quality-control problems. The company is shipping imperfect products and has to send engineers into the field to debug and repair them. The "obvious" answer is to implement more rigorous quality-control protocols. The opportunity might be to see how the start-up culture of moving fast, prototyping, and fixing mistakes needs to mature as the company has grown. The company does not just need better quality control; it needs a culture that moves more methodically, more strategically, and in a more integrated way. (See a complete annotated dialogue for this example at BregmanPartners.com/change.)

When my family moved from New York City to Savannah, Georgia, for a year, my wife, Eleanor, and I were looking forward to eating meals outdoors in our beautiful backyard (our energizing outcome). After three months, though, we had dined in the garden exactly one time. We were just too busy, exhausted, or lazy to schlep the utensils, plates, and food from the kitchen down to the garden (the problem). Rather than solving for busyness or laziness, our approach was to move the outdoor table ten feet closer to the house on the deck next to the exterior kitchen door (system change). After that, we ate every meal outside.

Now let's look at Ben and Ramona. While Ben's team is a great example of an upside in the downside opportunity, it is also a strong example of a system upgrade.

Dara helps Ben discover that getting rid of Ramona doesn't achieve his energizing outcome. It puts a Band-Aid on one part of the dysfunctional system without upgrading the system. A Ramona-less team, it turns out, is even more dysfunctional than what they have now, even though there's less tension and fewer hurt feelings.

Ramona's boldness represents a chance to create a culture of communication that supports a high-performing system: safety, respect, courage, and a willingness to speak and hear truth.

Dara helps Ben get there by asking for specifics about the ideal outcome.

BEN: Yes. Removing her might make it worse. She brings a quality of gutsiness that our team—again, me included—really needs.

DARA: That's so interesting. Given that, what would your high-performing team look and sound like?

BEN: They'd be as sensitive as me, and as brave as Ramona.

DARA: As sensitive as you and as brave as Ramona. That's compelling. And I can feel your excitement. Sensitive and brave at the same time?

BEN: More or less. If Ramona could just learn to speak her mind without alienating the rest of us, and the rest of us could learn to speak honestly and raise important issues, then we'd really get somewhere.

Ramona's problematic behavior is still an obstacle; it's important not to forget about this because it's part of what

Ben has to deal with. But it's also a doorway to a new outcome that's much bigger than the problem. Here's how Dara
helps drive that point home.

DARA:	So while Ramona's the problem . . .
BEN:	She holds a key piece of the solution.
DARA:	So can I rephrase what we're going for here?
BEN:	Yes, please.
DARA:	In order to achieve a high-performing team, you want to create a culture where everyone speaks their truth with care and sensitivity and commits to speaking, listening, and being open to hard truths for the sake of the team, the best outcomes, and their own growth and development. Did I get that right?
BEN:	Yes, totally. Now I'm actually kind of excited about building that high-performing team because I see that I've got all the pieces already. And yes, Ramona is part of the problem, but not the whole problem. I'm part of the problem too—as are the others on the team. And, together, we're the solution. I just have to figure out how to integrate those pieces.
DARA:	That does sound exciting.
BEN:	It's like we have two completely different cultures on the team—ours and Ramona's. Neither is right or wrong. Both are necessary for high perfor-mance. So how do I merge them?

What Ben ends up with, in essence, is a much more
interesting, exciting, and useful opportunity: how to merge
Ramona's behavior with that of the rest of the team so they
can create a team culture that is both caring and brave, attend-
ing to relationships and results.

Recall the initial problem Ben brought to Dara: to get Ramona to stop bossing people around.

Why is the integration of caring and bravery such a more interesting opportunity than the problem "Ramona bosses everyone around"? Let's recall the four powers of change: ownership, independent capability, emotional courage, and future-proofing.

First, when the problem is Ramona's behavior, no one else has to take ownership. There's nothing for anyone else to do. When the opportunity involves team dynamics, now everyone on the team has to (or "gets to") take ownership of the team culture and the outcomes it produces.

Second, Ramona—and the entire team—will increase their independent capability. All of them will get better at communicating.

Third, the changes the team members are facing—to risk hurting feelings by speaking more boldly—require (and therefore develop) emotional courage.

Fourth, the solution develops a stronger, more capable system. And improving a system makes it more resilient to future shocks.

Look for opportunities to increase ownership, build independent capability, practice emotional courage, and future-proof an individual and/or system. That way the change will not only happen, but it will stick. And the person or people involved will be well equipped to grow further, achieve more, and move through future obstacles in their path.

Once the system is stronger, it will also be future-proofed. For example, if Amali, who has a tendency to give long-winded and boring presentations, joins the team next, the system will support her integration into the culture and the team will have the skills to give her feedback and help her improve. The team will also be looking for how Amali's attention to detail and methodical approach to communicating can make them better, even as they help her streamline and prioritize her own communications.

WHEN THE PROBLEM LOOKS LIKE A SKILLS GAP

Sometimes the problem appears to be nothing more than an individual skills gap. The person you're helping wants to improve their ability to project manage, lead a team, or give a presentation. While Ramona's issue is dysfunctional behavior, it looks like Ben simply needs to become a better leader. Maybe Dara could have saved a lot of time by giving Ben a book on leadership and called it a day.

Nope. Because here's the thing about persistent problems that look like a skills or knowledge gap: they probably aren't.

When someone wants to close a knowledge or skills gap, they take a course, or follow the steps in a self-help book, or watch a YouTube video. Many of the challenges we face are exactly this type of problem: getting better at some technical task or gaining new knowledge and experience. In those cases, closing the gap between where you are and where you want to be is straightforward.

One of the clues that someone is dealing with a developmental challenge is their frustration that the technical solutions that should work—and that they've been trying for a long time—aren't working. They know these technical solutions work in theory, and they work for other people, so they just keep hitting their head against the wall, hoping that the next time will be different.

The goal here is to recognize the opportunity at hand: not a "Do" opportunity, but a "Be" opportunity. Help your partner identify who they would have to *be* in order to effectively implement the technical solution that would work. Then the new, reframed problem becomes, "How do I close the gap between who I am now and who I need to be?"

Developmental challenges are often scary. One common response to a development challenge is "Well, that's just not me." Putting it that way takes away responsibility—if they can't change, then there's nothing to be done. Their growth is limited by their fixed self-definition.

Psychologist Carol Dweck writes about fixed versus growth mindsets in her book *Mindset*. Her research shows not only that growth mindsets (the belief that a person can change and develop their abilities) are much more empowering than fixed mindsets (the belief that a person's abilities or talents are fixed), but also that it's possible to shift from fixed to growth. (Listen to my interview with her at BregmanPartners.com/change.) As their supportive partner, you can help them do so in this step, by reframing their self-definition as a temporary state.

Resist the urge to argue with your partner's self-definition. All you will do is reinforce it.

Don't:

CARL: I can't raise that issue with Annika. I'm just not an assertive person.

LIZ: Sure you are

And don't agree with your partner either.

Don't:

CARL: I can't raise that issue with Annika. I'm just not an assertive person.

LIZ: Ain't that the truth!

Instead, acknowledge that your partner needs to grow in order to achieve their goal. If they cling to that self-definition completely, you can gently guide them to identify counterexamples.

Do:

CARL: I can't raise that issue with Annika. I'm just not an assertive person.

LIZ: It sounds like being that assertive would be new and unfamiliar to you.

CARL: Yes. I've never been like that, for as long as I can remember.

LIZ: Can you think of any time in your life when you did speak up, even though it might have been scary?

Even if their limiting self-definition is completely and unwaveringly true (in their eyes), keep them focused on the future, where the possibility of change exists.

Do:

CARL: Nope. I've always shied away from conflict, my whole life.

LIZ: Are you willing to try a new approach?

Listen for clues in your partner's words that point to an aspirational identity. Howie has a friend Ian who had been morbidly obese until he changed his diet and started running. He had lost 150 pounds in less than a year but had plateaued before reaching his goal weight. What he wanted, he said, was to lose 20 more pounds.

Do:

HOWIE: What makes you think that 20 pounds is the right number?

IAN: I'll be running my first ultra-marathon in a few months, and I want to be athletically fit for it.

HOWIE: So what you really want here is to become an athlete?

IAN: Yes, that's right! During my last race, I real-
              ized that I needed to drop these extra pounds to
              become a better runner.

The reframe from "not being obese" to "being an athlete" led to a new approach to weight loss that was far more effective and sustainable than what Ian had been doing before. Ian confessed that despite his remarkable weight loss success, he still saw himself as an obese person, struggling every day not to slip back into his old habits. Had Ian merely solved the presenting problem (losing 20 pounds), he'd still be that formerly obese person, battling his true nature at every meal and during every workout.

Howie helped Ian identify a new opportunity: how to live like an athlete. (You can listen to the actual conversation at BregmanPartners.com/change.) And solving that problem both dealt with the 20 extra pounds and got Ian to a new and better place in his life.

In this example, Howie offered a theory ("You want to become an athlete") for Ian to consider. By posing it as a question (rising intonation at the end), Howie gave Ian implicit permission to reject it. Another way to do this is to explicitly state that it's a theory you want to check with them.

That might sound like any of the following:

> "I have an idea I'd like to run by you. It sounds like what you really want is to become an athlete. Does that sound right?"

> "I'm curious about something. I think what I heard was, you really want to become an athlete. Does that resonate?"

> "It seems like your big goal is not just to lose 20 pounds, but actually to become an athlete. What do you think?"

THE OPPORTUNITY IN A DYSFUNCTIONAL HABIT

When your partner's problem is a bad habit, resist the impulse to address that habit head-on.

Don't:

ME: My diet is terrible these days. I'm eating way too much sugar.

HOWIE: One strategy is to replace the sugary dessert with a piece of fruit.

This approach fails on three fronts. First, it's advice and positions Howie as a critic, not an ally. Second, I already know this. I tried dozens of strategies to stop eating sugar, and they all work—until they don't. Third, it misses the opportunity for growth.

Another common approach is to ask questions designed to increase your partner's motivation to change, either by focusing them on the negative consequences of the behavior or by focusing them on the good things they would get by changing the behavior. This approach, known in the health field as "motivational interviewing," has its place: when your partner really isn't motivated to change.

Generally Don't:

ME: My diet is terrible these days. I'm eating way too much sugar.

HOWIE: How is that negatively impacting your life?

ME: I've gained 10 pounds, I'm sluggish in the afternoons, and I don't want to develop some chronic disease.

HOWIE: What would your life be like if you could totally beat this sugar habit?

ME: I'd have more energy, better focus, and I'd feel better in my body.

Asking about the consequences, negative or positive, seems benign and can be useful if the issue is motivation. The important thing, however, is to notice the assumption baked into the question: If the other person were just motivated enough, they would stop. So we get them to focus on the bad consequences they want to avoid and the good consequences they want to experience.

Organizational psychologist Adam Grant points out that motivational interviewing can be an effective part of change, but only when you ask the questions out of genuine curiosity. That is, you might have an exchange like the one preceding when asking about what's happening now, when you truly want to understand how your partner relates to the problem. But don't do it to "motivate" your partner to change by getting them to say how terrible it is and how wonderful it would be to not have the problem.

Here's the thing: when people feel stuck, motivation is almost never the problem. I already feel bad enough about my sugar habit. I know that it's bad in the long run, so rubbing my nose in it won't bring about meaningful change. As I confessed earlier, that just makes me want to eat more sugar in a gesture of defiance or as a source of comfort.

Instead, turn motivational interviewing on its head.

Rather than trying to increase the person's awareness about why they want to make the change (which, in all likelihood, they already know), increase their awareness about what's driving their non-change.

Reframe the problem into an opportunity by asking what's functional about the behavior. What benefit do they get from it? Even our "worst" habits solve some problem in the short run; otherwise, we wouldn't be tempted to engage in them.

You can flesh out the opportunity by exploring a powerful question: "What's good about your current habit/behavior?"

In other words, "What purpose does it serve? Why are you doing it?"

You want your partner to be able to recognize how a "bad" habit or other dysfunctional behavior actually does something for them. Maybe it makes them feel better in the moment, as it's happening, even if the long-term costs are significant.

Drugs can temporarily lift us from despair to euphoria, or at least numbness. Gossip can help us connect with others. Criticizing others drowns out our painfully negative self-judgments.

The problem with these habits is that they invariably mask, rather than solve, the underlying issue. And that's also why they can be so useful as we help people change: They shine a light on those deeper problems that are actually opportunities for growth.

Since we're so used to feeling bad about our "bad" habits, asking what's good about them can interrupt fixed patterns of thinking quite powerfully. This move is so effective because we're expecting the opposite, a question about the negative consequences of the behavior.

Do:

ME: My diet is terrible these days. I'm eating way too much sugar.

HOWIE: I get why that's a problem for you. But, I'm curious, what's good about sugar? What does it do for you? How do you feel at the moment you begin to eat a sweet dessert?

ME: Excited. Alive. Fun. Childlike. Free. Energized.

HOWIE: How effective is sugar in keeping you feeling those things, in the short and long term?

ME: Terrible in the long term. It just makes me more
           tired and more dependent on sugar. I feel old, a
           little depressed even, low energy, and annoyed.
           Also I feel physically bad. And I hate that I can't
           control myself.

HOWIE: So let me share my bias here: If you need sugar
           to feel energized, then the problem isn't the
           sugar. It's the fact that you aren't managing
           your energy effectively. Would you be open to
           thinking about more effective ways to manage
           your energy?

The problem is no longer my sugar habit, but how to act in a way that keeps me energized. Now we can talk about sleep hygiene, regular work breaks, meditating, taking naps, replenishing energy with alone time or in the company of others, and other strategies as potential solutions to the more fundamental problem that sugar consumption was masking.

Many annoying workplace behaviors operate just like sugar—they are habits that solve a real problem in a short-term and suboptimal way. The person who is always trying to prove that they're smarter than everyone else is seeking validation. They want to be esteemed by the group, a valid human need. The person who's always interrupting is seeking significance or wants to make an impact. Again, a valid need.

The opportunity is to identify and positively address the valid, underlying need. The person who wants to be esteemed can actively seek feedback from their manager and peers and earn their regard through effort and contribution. The person seeking significance can find out what needs are currently going unmet and proactively address them.

THE OPPORTUNITY IN FEAR

Often, people are stuck because there's a risk they're unwilling to take. They're afraid—which, from an opportunity standpoint, is a *great* thing.

That's because fear is always an opportunity to practice—and consequently develop—courage. In fact, we can't develop our courage in the absence of fear. And developing courage is what enables us to take advantage of new opportunities.

Don't try to minimize your partner's fear or talk them out of it.

Don't:

VICKY: My boss keeps telling me that I have to contribute more in meetings, but I always stop myself from speaking because I think they all know more than I do.

LEANDRO: Well, that's just silly. You're the most experienced member of the team, and they all know it.

The reframe here is simple. Instead of addressing the details of the dysfunctional behavior, explore what they are trying to protect themselves from. Stay curious. What are they afraid will happen? What are they afraid of feeling?

Do:

VICKY: My boss keeps telling me that I have to contribute more in meetings, but I always stop myself from speaking because I think they all know more than I do.

LEANDRO: What do you think might happen if you spoke up in a meeting?

VICKY: Everyone might realize what an idiot I am.

Once your partner identifies their fear, you've found a stellar opportunity: to act *in the face of that fear*. It may not be the only opportunity, but it's a great place to start.

A bonus step here is to probe for a pattern. Someone with a fear of making a fool of themselves in a particular work meeting most likely self-censors their words and actions in other venues—professional and personal.

Do:

LEANDRO: Is this a familiar feeling? Are there other instances at work or other areas of your life where fear of what others will think of you gets in the way of something you care about?

VICKY: Yes, my brothers and I are trying to help our mother sell her house, and I bite my tongue a lot, even though I have the most experience with that sort of thing.

LEANDRO: Anywhere else?

If your partner says no, that's fine. Simply continue the process by assessing if the fear is entirely rational.

LEANDRO: I'm hearing that staying quiet in meetings is a strategy for appearing competent to your colleagues. Does that sound right?

VICKY: Yes, that's it.

LEANDRO: So, I want to check in with you about something. Do you have useful things to say during meetings that you don't share?

VICKY: I think so. But then I think, "They're all so smart, they must have thought of this already," and I shut up.

LEANDRO: And have they always thought of it already? Or have there been times when you had an idea that nobody else had?

VICKY: Sometimes they get there, but honestly, I could have gotten us there faster. Other times I leave the meeting and kick myself because I stayed quiet and the idea never came out—and I think we end up with a suboptimal solution.

LEANDRO: So this isn't an issue of lack of knowledge, skills, or relevant experience, right?

This is an important step, because you don't want to assume that the fear is completely unfounded. Sometimes fears are rational, and protective, and should be honored. In this case, it was unlikely, since Vicky's boss was encouraging her to contribute more.

Once you've determined that the problematic behavior is a product of an unuseful fear, the next step is to share your view that the fear is an opportunity for growth.

Do:

VICKY: Right, I keep quiet because I'm afraid of making a fool of myself. How do I get rid of that fear?

LEANDRO: You keep quiet in meetings because you're afraid of what other people will think, and that behavior is actually getting in the way of you contributing to the team. Assuming you continue to rise within this organization, you'll always face situations where you'll want to keep quiet because you think you're in over your head. Does that sound right?

VICKY: Yes, that's right.

LEANDRO: OK, let me share my bias here. So my take is that you have a great opportunity here. People often think they need to totally overcome a fear in order to act, but the way I see it, that's a mistake. The best—and probably only—way to overcome a fear is to act while you're feeling the fear. For you, that would mean showing up and speaking out even while you're scared of their disapproval. Is that something you'd like to work on?

VICKY: Yes, absolutely.

Finding an opportunity in fear checks all the boxes of change. People who face their fears take ownership, reclaiming their lives from the limitations that those fears impose. They develop independent capability as they take new and more empowered actions, which also develops their emotional courage. And they future-proof by practicing an approach that they can draw upon every time they face the limitations of a new fear.

CHAPTER 22

HOW NOT TO GET DISTRACTED

KEEP YOUR GPS ON

It's easy to get distracted from your objectives. When things get hard or complicated or a little confusing, distractions are tempting. They protect us from feeling discomfort.

The Opportunity step may be uncomfortable for your conversation partner because it's the point where they imagine a new direction—the point of forward movement where they let go of the comfort of resignation to an unsolvable problem and grab hold of the discomfort of trying again. Trying something new can be scary, especially when it requires shifting from helpless victim to accountable actor.

Because it's scary, your partner may pursue distractions—red herrings that may take you off your game so they can avoid taking a risk. They're not doing it maliciously or even on purpose. But the result will be a frustrating conversation that keeps them stuck. You need to keep them on track.

Don't take the bait: don't indulge, and don't argue. Both strategies will bring you to dead ends, or loops where you go round and round, failing to gain traction.

Instead, simply acknowledge them and move on. Here's how to bypass the most common distractions.

DISTRACTION: BLAMING OTHERS

One way our conversation partner can distract us from the process of change is by criticizing the people around them: The boss is an idiot. The teammates are jerks. The spouse is a nag. The kids are rude.

When they blame someone else, they're off the hook. "There's nothing I can do, because as everyone knows, you can't change other people." And while we know that you *can* change other people, you can't do it as a critic. Blame doesn't work.

Just as you strive to be an ally to the person you're helping to change, you also want to guide them to go from critic to ally of the people that *they* want to change.

When they tell you that their team is failing because Ramona is a jerk, don't argue, and don't try to solve for Ramona's jerkiness. Don't try to get them to empathize with Ramona either; you'll meet a lot of resistance.

And here's the main point: it isn't necessary. In fact, any evaluation of Ramona's behavior or personality is a distraction. It doesn't matter to you if she's a jerk or not; that's irrelevant. The important point here is the energizing outcome: what the person is trying to accomplish. Counterintuitively, here's where you get *un*curious about Ramona.

Don't:

BEN: Honestly, Ramona is just being a jerk to everyone on the team.

DARA: How is she being a jerk?

There's no need to solve for Ramona being a jerk. Instead, simply explore how Ramona's behavior is supporting or sabotaging the outcome they want.

Do:

BEN: Honestly, Ramona is just being a jerk to everyone
         on the team.

DARA: Let's go back to what you're trying to accomplish
         with this team, and then look more broadly at
         what's getting in the way of getting there—Ramona
         and anything else.

You can be explicit about it: "I don't want to get distracted
by Ramona. Let's talk about what you're trying to accomplish
and what's getting in the way."

DISTRACTION: SELF-CRITICISM

Sometimes your partner directs blame inward, at themselves.
While this can look like they're taking responsibility, it's actually
a subtle way of avoiding it. Their attention and energy focus
on their shortcomings, rather than on what they could do differently. Self-criticism replaces action far more often than it
precedes it.

Don't argue with their self-blame, no matter how tempting. All you'll do is reinforce it, as their mind goes into over-
drive looking for proof to override your objections. And you'll
break rapport, taking an adversarial stance rather than that of
a partner.

Don't:

COLIN: I want to be a more encouraging team member,
           but I'm just grumpy by nature.

DANIELLE: Oh come on, you're not any grumpier than
           anyone else.

COLIN: That's not true—you don't know what goes
           on in my head most of the time. It's like Fight
           Club in there.

And don't try to solve for their self-blame either. Not for grumpiness, or laziness, or lack of motivation, or inability to focus, or any other interpretation that sees a repeated behavior as an unchangeable trait. When you focus on the trait, you're just reinforcing it as the limiting factor.

Don't:

COLIN: I want to be a more encouraging team member, but I'm just grumpy by nature.

DANIELLE: Do you meditate in the morning? I find that 10 minutes of just watching my thoughts helps me observe my negative thoughts without acting on them.

And don't accuse them of using self-blame to avoid accountability.

Don't:

COLIN: I want to be a more encouraging team member, but I'm just grumpy by nature.

DANIELLE: When you call yourself "grumpy," you're just making an excuse for yourself. Saying that, since that's how you are, you aren't responsible for changing.

Instead—and this is incredibly counterintuitive—simply ignore the bait entirely. View it, for now, as completely beside the point.

Focus instead on action: What would they do if they didn't have this blameworthy trait? If they could wave a magic wand and no longer be grumpy, or lazy, or unmotivated—what would that look like?

Do:

COLIN: I want to be a more encouraging team member, but I'm just grumpy by nature.

DANIELLE: If you weren't grumpy, how would you act that would be more encouraging toward your team members? What would that look like?

COLIN: When they come to me with an idea that isn't fully formed, I'd brainstorm with them instead of shooting it down.

The "grumpy" label wasn't a path to a solution; it was a distraction. Once neutralized, Colin is now oriented toward a new problem to solve: developing a brainstorming habit to replace a criticism habit.

Chances are that Colin's grumpiness is rooted in some fear: fear of looking weak and indecisive, fear of not being seen as the smartest person in the room, and so on. As Danielle continues to work with Colin on finding opportunities to brainstorm, they'll find that his secondary opportunity is to act generously and collaboratively while feeling that fear.

DISTRACTION: FEAR THAT THE FUTURE WILL ECHO THE PAST

A sneaky and very common form of self-criticism is when people resign themselves to repeating their past—when they assume that their past performance immutably determines their future performance. *If I've always lost my temper in a given situation, I always will*, the thinking goes.

These self-definitions arise when people define themselves rigidly. When they look at the past and focus on their failures. When they compare their actions to some "ideal" way to behave. When they speedily reject future actions that contradict their self-image. "That's not me," they'll tell you when imagining asking for a raise, getting up 30 minutes early to exercise, or stepping up to lead a project team.

Again, don't argue, and don't fall for the trap of trying to change a trait they believe is unchangeable. Again, reframe from the problem ("I'll never change") to the opportunity (what the change would look like if it were to occur).

HOW TO BECOME DISTRACTION-PROOF: EMOTIONAL COURAGE

The magic of the Opportunity step is to transform your partner's negative or defensive or problem-focused mindset into a positive, discovery-based, and opportunity-focused one—which means you have to lead with a positive mental attitude yourself. That's why you have to drop your own frustration, anger, or sadness before you engage. Your own negative mindset serves only to reinforce their defensive, uncreative, brittle obsession with their problem.

Of course, you can't turn off negative emotions on command. Pretending they don't exist doesn't work. Indulging them doesn't make them go away; to the contrary, it feeds them. The only way through is through: as you saw in the chapter on preparing yourself for the conversation, you have to feel those emotions fully, acknowledge them, and translate them into your care for your conversation partner and for a positive outcome. This step provides the payoff for all that emotional courage work by giving them the space to move into a generative Opportunity frame of mind.

STEP 4

CREATE A LEVEL-10 PLAN

Step 1: Ally → Step 2: Outcome → Step 3: Opportunity → **Step 4: Plan**

CHAPTER 23

CRAFT THE PLAN

MOVE FROM INSIGHT TO TRACTION

It's thrilling to transform a frustrating problem into an exciting opportunity to achieve an energizing outcome.

That's what we've accomplished so far in the first three steps of the change process. Ben is ready to create a new, dynamic high-performing team, leveraging Ramona's boldness and the rest of the team's sweetness. Ben sees things he didn't see before. His unsolvable problem is now a springboard to greater success. He's optimistic, clear, and focused.

What about the person you're helping to change? You'll lead them to this same place as you bring them through the three steps we've just covered. They will be excited and full of potential too.

Insights are great, but they aren't sufficient. Your job now is to guide your partner to operationalize those insights—to get *traction* and to create a specific, time-bound plan to use the opportunity to achieve the outcome. It doesn't have to be the *right* or *perfect* plan. It just has to be one that has a reasonable chance of success and from which they can learn and improve.

Traction comes from acting, learning, adjusting, and acting again. Think of your plan as an experiment designed to provide feedback and focus to the next round of action.

Your Partner has three tasks in Step 4: **Identify Options**, **Choose**, and **Commit**.

First, you'll help your partner identify at least three options to capitalize on the opportunity you've just uncovered.

Second, you'll guide them to choose from those options to create a plan.

Third, you'll support them in committing to clear actions and deadlines—what they are going to do, how, and when.

The end result of Step 4 is a clear and specific Level-10 plan, a plan that when you ask your partner, "How confident are you, on a scale from 1 to 10, that you will carry out this plan?" they answer, "10!"

They will own and commit to it because they developed it themselves.

They will grow their independent capability as they experiment with new behaviors, changing what they're saying or doing to achieve their energizing outcome.

They will tap into and grow their emotional courage as they risk new approaches and role-play tough scenarios.

And they will emerge with a process—this process—that they can go through again and again, future-proofing them in the face of new challenges.

In the next three chapters, we'll explore each of the three tasks in depth.

CHAPTER 24

TASK 1: IDENTIFY OPTIONS

LET'S PUT THAT ON THE LIST. WHAT ELSE MIGHT YOU TRY?

In the Identify Options task, you are going to get your partner's creative juices flowing so that they can come up with multiple possibilities for effective action to achieve their energizing outcome.

If they've been stuck, struggling with a problem for a long time, this is a chance for them to reclaim their agency. Often, you'll gently nudge them past the obvious solutions into new and exciting (sometimes scary) territory. Just as you grow muscles in the gym by exercising them to failure, you want to encourage your partner to exercise their creativity muscle slightly past the point of comfort.

Let's return to Dara and Ben to see how they identify options.

DARA: So given that opportunity, what might you try?

BEN: [*Chuckles*] Well, it's funny. Before we talked, the most obvious solution was to fire Ramona, or boot her from the team. Now that's not even on my list of options. It would miss the opportunity, and it wouldn't even get us close to the outcome of a high-performing team.

DARA: That's a great observation.

BEN: Well, one thing we could do is, HR has a 360 process that we've never done as a team. We could do it and use it as a way to talk together about our strengths and weaknesses as a team.

DARA: Are you writing these down?

BEN: Um . . . I am now.

DARA: What else might you try?

BEN: I guess one thing I could do is bring in an outside vendor who does team-building. We could take an assessment and then get some training. That would take the stress off me but it wouldn't be as cheap as me. [*Smiles*]

DARA: Cool. Let's play a little—what could you try if money weren't an issue? If you had an unlimited budget.

BEN: If we had the budget, I'd just hire coaches for everyone, including me.

DARA: Awesome! Anything else with an unlimited budget?

BEN: Nah, that would be the ultimate.

DARA: OK, so that's worth putting on the list. What else might you try here?

BEN: Well, I could be the bargain-counter coach, and give all my team members individual feedback about what they're doing well and what they need to work on.

DARA: Terrific. And let me ask you something. Before I do, I want to share my bias. Is that OK?

BEN: Sure.

DARA: Well, here's what I'm thinking. Your goal is to get Ramona and the rest of the team to work together, to combine their gifts and mitigate their weaknesses. Does that sound right?

BEN: Yes, totally.

DARA: OK, given that, my bias is that one of the things you want to do is help them talk to each other in a real and respectful way. So could one option be to have a team meeting in which you lay out essentially everything we've discovered here together. Openly and honestly? What's your reaction to that idea?

BEN: I think that would be awesome. It's just a bit scary. And I'm afraid Ramona might take it as us ganging up on her, you know, like the same dynamic we've been having up until now.

DARA: Is there anything you might try to say to Ramona prior to that meeting to put her at ease or make her more likely to engage?

BEN: I'm not sure.

DARA: If you could say anything to Ramona, with no negative consequences whatsoever, guaranteed, what might you say?

BEN: I'm not sure.

DARA: What's the scariest thing you could say to her?

BEN: You know, I realize that in my attempt to keep her from damaging the team's morale, I've been cutting her off. Pretty much silencing her, or trying to side-line her. Part of me actually wants to apologize to Ramona, but I'm afraid that she'll take that to mean she was right, and she won't change.

DARA: Let's hold off on critiquing the options. Right now, how about you add it as an option?

BEN: Sure. I'll write, "Apologize to Ramona."

DARA: OK—and let's play that one out a bit. What might you say in the conversation after apologizing?

BEN: Well, something like, "Ramona, you raise incredibly important issues that no one else has been willing to look at. The rest of us are very careful about how we talk to one another, and we're very good at keeping the peace, but we need your willingness to engage in difficult conversations. Are you open to feedback from the team about how to raise these issues in a way that feels safe, so we can hear them fully?"

DARA: Great. Anything else you might try?

BEN: That's a lot of options right there.

DARA: I agree. And they run the gamut. Great job. Should we make some choices and come up with a plan?

BEN: Yeah, let's do it.

We'll pause the dialogue here for now and explore a variety of ways to help your partner come up with great options.

TIPS TO HELP IDENTIFY OPTIONS

Sometimes identifying options just flows, with only the most minimal guidance on your part. At other times, your partner may struggle to exploit the opportunity in service of the outcome.

The important thing is to guide *them* to run with it, especially if you think you "know" the answer.

The inquiry that guides identifying options is straightforward: "How do you want to pursue this opportunity? What might you try?"

Don't:
"What do you want to do?"

Do:
"What might you try?"

Try is an important word here. You want to separate *brainstorming* (which is what we're doing when we identify options) from *deciding* (which happens in the next task, when we choose). When you ask your partner what they want to *try*, you're eliminating the need for commitment at this point.

You're also eliminating the need to come up with perfect options, those guaranteed to succeed.

Ben suggests apologizing to Ramona as a first step in rebuilding a relationship. Will this work? There is no way to know in advance. Ramona might react negatively to Ben's apology, rather than mirror his vulnerability.

It doesn't matter if the options are obviously great. Your goal at this point is to put as many options on the table as possible. When brainstorming, the quality of the eventual solution depends largely on the quantity of total solutions considered.

So when your partner comes up with an option, now is not the time to judge or evaluate it. Don't compare it to other options. Don't ask for a detailed explanation of how they would implement it. Don't stress-test it or plan for contingencies. Those responses discourage further brainstorming. Evaluation comes later.

Don't:

BEN: I could ask Ramona to create a presentation on how to disagree without being disagreeable.

DARA: Yeah, I suppose. [*Total lack of enthusiasm*] What else might you do?

BEN: [*Stony silence*]

Do:

BEN: I could ask Ramona to create a presentation on how to disagree without being disagreeable.

DARA: Great, let's put that on the list. What else might you try?

BEN: Well, I could . . .

Don't even express enthusiasm for an option. Praising an idea may feel like you're being encouraging, but you've actually just made it harder for them to share another one. You've still set yourself up as a critic and judge, rather than an ally. Now they'll start to self-censor, based on whether they think you will approve of the next one as much as the last. Instead, offer positive reinforcement, not for the quality of the idea, but for the fact that they came up with it.

Don't:

BEN: I could start by taking responsibility for my own contribution to this situation and apologize to Ramona for all the times I've tried to shut her down.

DARA: Oh my gosh, I love that so much. There's no way Ramona won't be moved by that. And what else could you try?

BEN: I dunno. That's my best idea.

Do:

BEN: I could start by taking responsibility for my own contribution to this situation and apologize to Ramona for all the times I've tried to shut her down.

DARA: Great, let's put that on the list. What else might you try?

BEN: Well, I could . . .

Your response to every option can be as simple as, "Great, let's put that on the list." In the dialogue, Dara nudges Ben to take responsibility for the list by asking him if he's writing the options down. That's his job, not Dara's. It's his plan. That move reinforces Ben's ownership of the opportunity and his need to take responsibility for achieving his energizing outcome.

WHAT ELSE?

After encouraging your partner to "Put it on the list," follow up with another question to keep the ball rolling: "What else might you try?"

It's OK at this point if the options are vague ("I could try collaborating with them"); you will pin down the details when you get them to choose and commit. For now, trust that whatever they suggest, in whatever language they use, means something sufficiently precise to them that you can work with it later.

It may be tempting to skip identifying multiple options and just choose a path forward. When someone achieves a new insight or perspective on a problem, they can get excited and even impatient. They may think they know exactly how to move forward. The danger, though, is that they miss out on great ideas because they jump too quickly on the first one.

So how many options should they identify? I aim for three or more. One isn't an option. Two may have them feeling stuck between a rock and a hard place. Three or more provides genuine choice, and the effort that goes into coming up with new and unfamiliar options usually rewards them with better ones that are more creative, more challenging, and more powerful.

WHAT ABOUT YODA?

The word *try* has gotten a bad rap in the self-help world, thanks to Yoda's admonition to Luke Skywalker in *The Empire Strikes Back*. When Yoda tells Luke to raise his X-wing fighter from the swamp of Dagobah, and Luke replies that he'll try, Yoga reprimands him: "Do, or do not. There is no try."

Yoda hears *try* as an expression of Luke's lack of commitment and lack of faith.

That use of the word *try* is not what I'm talking about here. When Luke says he'll try, he means that he'll attempt the feat, but doesn't really have much faith.

I mean *try* in a different sense: like when the waiter at that new restaurant recommends the spicy cauliflower wings: "Sure, I'll try them." *Try* as in, "I'll do it and see how it goes."

Try allows them to view the option as an experiment, which means it's not such a big deal if it doesn't work. There's always something to learn from a try that didn't work and always another option to try.

By talking about trying and experiments, you're also communicating that you're a dependable ally; your partner is not going to disappoint or disillusion you if this option doesn't succeed. It's about them, not you. You're there to help them achieve their energizing outcome.

HOW TO HELP GENERATE OPTIONS

Sometimes your partner will get stuck and won't be able to generate options on their own. Often, this is because their "inner critic," the part of their mind that wants to keep them safe by avoiding risk, filters out any suggestions that will push them out of their comfort zone.

One of the greatest gifts you can give them is space and encouragement to question—and defy—the part of their mind that's telling them, "Don't even consider that."

Following are several techniques for encouraging your partner to generate multiple options.

EXPAND OPTIONS BY LOWERING THE BAR
FOR SUCCESS

Take the pressure off your partner by reminding them that they're not looking for the "right" option here—just a number of them. Bad ideas, one-chance-in-a-million schemes, and outlandish escapades are all fine.

Don't:

BEN: I could apologize to Ramona in front of the team at our next meeting. Oh, man, I'm shaking just thinking about it.

DARA: That's a bit risky—what if it backfires?

BEN: Oh, you're right. Forget it.

Do:

BEN: I could apologize to Ramona in front of the team at our next meeting. Oh, man, I'm shaking just thinking about it.

DARA: That feels risky, huh? It's great that you're able to say it out loud. Let's put it on the list.

BEN: What if it backfires?

DARA: That's certainly a possibility. None of these options is guaranteed to work. We'll choose an option with a risk/reward ratio that you're comfortable with, and whatever happens, we'll learn something.

Another way to lower the bar for success is to ask the question: "What would you do if you didn't care whether you failed?"

EXPAND OPTIONS BY RECALLING PAST ATTEMPTS

Remind your partner of what they've already tried. Past attempts—whether successful or not—can provide insight on what might work going forward. The failed attempts can provide clues about what *not* to do and might suggest new paths forward by doing the opposite or simply a variation of the initial attempt. People often stop doing things that worked for a variety of reasons. It may be possible to incorporate a past strategy into the new plan.

EXPAND OPTIONS THROUGH WHAT-IFS

Sometimes people limit their thinking based on what they assume is possible. You can spur creativity through two different types of hypothetical questions.

The first type *removes* constraints. The second type *adds* constraints.

Dara used the first type in the conversation with Ben when she asked what he might try given an unlimited budget. When your partner is out of ideas, take away a limitation that you suspect might be curtailing their best thinking:

"What might you try if your budget were unlimited?"

"What could you attempt if you had all the time in the world?"

"What would you do if you were the only decision-maker here?"

"What would you do if you were sure your data were 100 percent accurate?"

How can *adding* constraints stimulate creativity? The history of entrepreneurship demonstrates that people can get very creative when resources are limited. When the obvious avenues are blocked, people are forced to come up with unconventional approaches that may prove far more elegant and effective than existing best practices.

Here's one example: Because of the pandemic, the Monkey Bar Gym in Madison, Wisconsin, was forced to close its facility. That's a constraint that could have shut down their business for good. What's a gym without a gym? But they chose a different option: They went online.

Co-owners Jon and Jessie Hinds now say they'll never go back to brick and mortar.

They're saving $180,000 per year in rent, accessing clients from around the world, and thanks to Zoom's gallery view, offering more personalization as they can give instant feedback on form to dozens of students at once. Their response to a massive constraint increased profits, improved the product, expanded their customer base, and reduced stress. Howie, one of those new clients, lives 1,000 miles away from their facility. He owes his new biceps to the power of constraints.

If not for the constraints created by the pandemic, Jon and Jessie Hinds would never have expanded their thinking—or their business.

When your partner is operating out of a stuck way of thinking, you can prime their creative pump by adding constraints:

"How would you approach this issue if you only had 15 minutes to deal with it?"

"What if you couldn't spend a single penny on the problem?"

"What if you couldn't remove Ramona from the team?"

EXPAND OPTIONS THROUGH EMOTIONAL COURAGE CHALLENGES

Sometimes your partner will come up with options that lack variety and boldness. Is that okay, or should you push them to expand their range of options? The answer is, it depends.

Ultimately, your goal is to come up with a plan that offers a reasonable probability of success. If the magic of the new opportunity has suddenly opened up a whole new set of possibilities, they don't necessarily have to be "stretches" for your partner.

If, on the other hand, one of the opportunities is for them to develop their emotional courage muscle—to take more risks and do things that feel uncomfortable—then it's almost always fruitful to encourage them to think more broadly, bypassing the mental filter that screens out possibilities that don't feel "like them."

When there's an emotional courage component to the opportunity, try asking some variant of the question, "What's the scariest thing you could try here?" That question is a great pattern interrupter because it's explicitly asking your partner to imagine an action beyond the scope of anything they would ordinarily consider.

Other questions to help your partner extend their creative planning into emotional courage territory include the following:

"What's an action someone would least expect from you?"

"What's completely off the table?"

"What is absolutely 'undiscussable' here?"

"What's a truth that nobody's saying?"

"If you had an invisibility cloak and you could act or speak without being seen or recognized, what might you try?"

EXPAND OPTIONS THROUGH "OPPOSITE DAY" QUESTIONS

Another way to bust through limiting assumptions is to ask questions to identify options, not with the highest, but with the *lowest* probability of success. These "Opposite Day" questions can expand creativity in a number of ways.

First, they can be funny. Researchers Mark Beeman and John Kounios found that people were 20 percent better at solving creative word problems after watching a short Robin Williams comedy clip.

Second, they give your partner explicit permission to come up with "stupid" answers, which lowers the pressure and thus encourages risk-taking.

Third, often the opposite of a "stupid" idea is a good one. Back in the day, when Howie consulted with marketing clients who were completely stumped on how to increase website conversion rates, he'd remind them of the action they wanted visitors to take on a particular page, and then ask, "How could we make it *less* likely that they'd take that action?" They'd immediately be full of ideas: decrease the font of the key statements, move the "Subscribe" button below the fold, promise to spam anyone who entered their email, and so on. After a few minutes of this ridiculous exercise, the client had a long list of improvements, simply enacting the opposite of what they had just brainstormed.

Some ways to phrase the "Opposite Day" questions include the following:

"What definitely wouldn't work here?"

"What would be the worst way to approach this?"

"What option would provide the least value for the greatest effort?"

"How could you make the problem worse?"

EXPAND OPTIONS THROUGH LADDERING

Sometimes your partner's creativity can get hamstrung by the magnitude of the problem or opportunity. They may be trying to solve the whole thing, once and for all, in a single bound. One way to help them break free from all-or-nothing thinking is to introduce the concept of "laddering"—that is, breaking big climbs into modest, manageable steps.

You can help your partner identify rungs on the ladder in a few different ways.

One approach is to look at the energizing outcome as a project goal and list out the steps required to achieve it. Then order the steps chronologically, breaking them into achievable one-at-a-time chunks.

If the energizing outcome is to write a book, the first rung might be to write an outline or a description of the ideal reader (in this case, that's you, by the way) or a list of questions you want the book to answer. If the energizing outcome is Couch to 5k, the first step might be to be able to jog from one lamppost to another without stopping to walk.

A great "laddering" question is "What can you try this week to get into a better position next week?"

Another approach is to identify ladder steps based on difficulty. Just as someone who wants to get stronger will work with increasingly heavy weights as they increase their capacity using lighter ones, your partner can start with easier actions to build their skill and confidence for harder ones.

To someone who is afraid of public speaking, for example, raising their hand and speaking at the full company town hall may be too daunting to even consider. Speaking at a team meeting, or even a family reunion via video conferencing, might feel more doable.

A third approach is particularly effective if the goal is to change an ingrained pattern of behavior. In that case, they can ladder by picking specific moments and situations, rather than attempting a 24/7 transformation.

For example, taking a deep breath and pausing before speaking might be extremely difficult at night after a long day's work when a young child is being particularly unreasonable and demanding. But that same behavior might be much easier during a 10 a.m. conference call with an annoying colleague. By practicing during the conference call, your partner can develop habits and muscles that can be deployed in ever more challenging situations, including—eventually—evenings at home.

HOW TO SUGGEST OPTIONS

Sometimes your partner will have no idea what to do and may come up blank. Or you may want to share an idea of your own. In those cases, you may offer your own suggestions.

There are three rules to making a suggestion:

1. Make the suggestion, rather than trying to lead your partner to the idea.
2. Introduce the suggestion with your reason for raising it: "Based on my experience . . ." or "My bias is that. . . ."
3. Ask for their reaction in a way that allows them to reject it without penalty.

Don't:

DARA: So remind me of the opportunity.

BEN: To combine gifts and mitigate weaknesses in pursuit of great communication and high performance.

DARA: So given that, does giving individual feedback seem like the best way of getting them to collaborate?

BEN: No, I guess not . . .

DARA: So what might be a more effective strategy to foster honest and caring communication among your team?

BEN: [*A bit annoyed at being "led" to an answer*] Well, I guess to get everyone in the same room.

DARA: Great! Let's put that on the list.

BEN: Fine. [*But not really fine; kind of resentful, actually*]

Do:

DARA: I want to share my bias. Is that OK?

BEN: Sure.

DARA: Well, here's what I'm thinking. Your goal is to get Ramona and the rest of the team to work together, to combine their gifts and mitigate their weaknesses. Does that sound right?

BEN: Yes, totally.

DARA: OK, given that, my bias is that one of the things you want to do is help them talk to each other in a real and respectful way. So one option could be to have a team meeting in which you lay out essentially everything we've discovered here together. Openly and honestly. What's your reaction to that idea?

BEN: I think that would be awesome. It's just a bit scary. And I'm afraid Ramona might take it as us ganging up on her, you know, like the same dynamic we've been having up till now.

You're not trying to convince them that you're right. In fact, having your partner disagree with your directive comment can be more empowering than having them come up with their own. If their response is "That won't work," you can honestly reply with heartfelt enthusiasm: "Great! What about that specifically won't work?" Asking what specifically won't work about an option gives your partner something tangible to wrestle with, which often helps them find the next step forward.

When they reject a suggestion, there are three possibilities. First, you can learn something important that can help identify other, better options.

DARA: So I want to offer a suggestion here. What if you started the process by apologizing to Ramona for the times you've cut her off when she was trying to contribute?

BEN: No way. That would never work.

DARA: Great! What about that specifically wouldn't work?

BEN: She'd hear, "You've been right and I've been wrong." It would just reinforce her sense of victimhood, of being punished for having common sense and courage. I'm worried that she'll just lord it over me.

DARA: I'm curious—have you had experience apologizing to Ramona and having her lord it over you afterwards?

BEN: Actually, yes. Early on I apologized for a hurtful comment I'd made, and she kept bringing it up in meetings. I won't make that mistake again.

DARA: Gotcha. Well, that's really good information to keep in mind as we explore what might work here.

Second, they may realize that their objection is based on an unexamined assumption, and they might achieve a breakthrough by questioning that assumption.

DARA: I'm curious—have you had experience apologizing to Ramona and having her lord it over you afterwards?

BEN: No, but my mother used to do that whenever I apologized.

DARA: Huh—that's interesting. I'm curious—given that Ramona isn't your mother, is it worth keeping this as an option to explore?

BEN: Yeah, now that I hear myself, I'm clearly making assumptions about Ramona based on totally irrelevant experiences.

Third, you can demonstrate your support—and your stance as their ally—by simply being fine with their rejection of your suggestion.

DARA: So I want to offer a suggestion here. What if you
        started the process by apologizing to Ramona for
        the times you've cut her off when she was trying to
        contribute?

BEN: Absolutely not.

DARA: Cool. Let's take that off the table.

You can be direct here, but it's important to do it care-fully. Make sure you're suggesting rather than instructing. Use phrases like, "What do you think about . . ." and "So what about this . . ." and "Here's an idea."

Pay close attention to their body language, tone of voice, and general demeanor when you offer options. You can usu-ally detect a change of energy—positive or negative—when a suggestion of yours has an impact one way or another.

Once they've come up with three or more options, you can now move to the second task of Step 4: helping them choose.

CHAPTER 25

TASK 2: CHOOSE THE PATH FORWARD

IF YOU DID KNOW, WHAT WOULD IT BE?

When you were identifying options, you asked your partner to withhold judgment and come up with lots of ideas. Now's the time to evaluate the options and choose a path forward with a reasonable probability of success.

It's worth emphasizing again that **your partner needs to guide this part of the process**.

Their independent choice is critical to their ownership of the plan and, therefore, to their willingness to follow through on it.

Let's see how this plays out with Dara and Ben.

DARA: You've got a great set of options here. Now you can choose how to move forward. Look at them individually or combine them in different ways. Given everything that's on the table, what do you want to do that would feel exciting?

BEN: I think the team meeting where we air everything is probably the key step.

DARA: Awesome. Take me there. How do you kick things off? Let's play it out.

BEN: It's our usual Tuesday morning meeting in the conference room. The whole team is there. I start the meeting by saying, "Welcome, everyone. Today I want us to mold ourselves into a high-performing team." [*Pauses*] Oh, man. That sounds so clichéd. Eyes will roll—including mine.

DARA: Is that a problem?

BEN: Yeah, I think I'll lose them if I don't start by acknowledging what's been happening.

DARA: So what might you say instead?

BEN: What if I just lead with the punchline? "We've got tremendous potential on this team, and the ways we're communicating with each other—and failing to communicate—are getting in the way. We're all aware of it, and today I want to acknowledge it and get everyone's help in addressing and fixing it." Wow. That felt good. And scary.

DARA: Good and scary—that's an encouraging combination from my perspective. It sounds like you think it has a good chance of success, and it will stretch you in a way you want to be stretched—to tell your truth even if it's uncomfortable for you and others.

BEN: Yeah, I think so.

DARA: So let's play this out. What do you think will happen after you kick off the meeting that way? What might Ramona do or say?

BEN: Hmm. She might take it as a personal attack. Like everyone knows that she's the squeaky wheel and that talking about the team's communication problem is just a coded way of criticizing her.

DARA: Given that you want Ramona to be part of the solution, what might you do to get her to help instead of retreating into defensiveness?

BEN: I think I'd better talk with her first.

DARA: What do you want that conversation to accomplish?

BEN: I want her to see herself as a leader and to take responsibility for changing her tone to be a more effective leader. I also want her to know that I appreciate her intentions, even though we've had a rough relationship.

DARA: What part of that do you think she needs to hear first?

BEN: I don't think she'll take kindly to me asking her to be more of a leader and to change her tone until I've—well, I'll say it—acknowledged how I've treated her.

DARA: What might that sound like? How would you start the conversation?

BEN: Well, it won't be a straight up apology. I don't want to give up my power to her, and that's how she'll read it.

DARA: What's the truth that you'd like her to know?

BEN: Basically, that a lot of what she's been trying to do for the team is stuff that we need, and I recognize that I've reacted poorly to it. And I'd like her to have more impact on the team, rather than less.

DARA: Great. Can you imagine saying that to her?

BEN: Yes, absolutely. I can have that conversation with her this afternoon.

DARA: What might she say?

BEN: Well, she'll be gruff, and probably suspicious of my motives, and I can't say I blame her. But she'll want specifics. Like, "OK, how do you want me to have more impact? Are you going to have my back now, or do I have to change?"

DARA: What's your answer?

BEN: "Ramona, I see now that your willingness to experience conflict for the sake of our success is something that the rest of us really need. You point out risks that we tend to ignore. And we—and I'm including myself here—have to be willing to engage in those conversations if we want to achieve our potential. At the same time, the way you're currently doing it is turning people off. Are you open to having a conversation about how we can incorporate your ability to raise tough issues into a team that still feels like a place where people feel respected and cared for?"

DARA: How do you feel when you hear yourself say that?

BEN: It finally feels like the truth. It's caring, and courageous. I guess I'm modeling what I want our team culture to be, aren't I? [*Smiles*] If she says yes, she's open to that, then I guess my next step is to ask her to help me plan the team meeting to start that process.

DARA: What if she says no?

BEN: [*Pauses*]

DARA: [*Silence*]

BEN: [*Finally*] Then I thank her for being honest with me. And repeat that I think she could be a positive contributor—a leader—and ask her what would have to change for her to reconsider. If she says, "Nothing," then I can ask how she'd like to proceed. Does she want the status quo to continue, or would she prefer some other future? And maybe we have our breakup right then and there. But you know what—I will already be a different kind of leader at that point, just from having had the courage to bring up the issue directly. So even if she leaves, I think the team can still change in positive ways.

DARA: That sounds really great.

Let's pause and use this dialogue to explore how to help your partner choose their path forward.

ASK FOR DETAILS

Initiate the Choose task by asking your partner what they want to do to achieve their energizing outcome. I often ask, "What do you want to do that would feel exciting?"— especially when there's an opportunity for emotional courage.

Once your partner has selected an option, or a combination of options, ask them to get specific.

DARA: You've got a great set of options here. Now you can choose how to move forward. Look at them individually, or combine them in different ways. Given your desire for a high-performing team, and everything that's on the table, what do you want to do that would feel exciting?

BEN: I think the team meeting where we air everything is probably the key step.

DARA: Awesome. Take me there. How do you kick things off? Let's play it out.

BEN: It's our usual Tuesday morning meeting in the conference room. The whole team is there. I start the meeting by saying, "Welcome, everyone. Today I want us to mold ourselves into a high-performing team." [*Pauses*] Oh, man. That sounds so clichéd. Eyes will roll—including mine.

IDENTIFY AND EXPLORE RISKS

As long as Ben remains vague about his plan ("a team meeting"), he can't evaluate it accurately. By asking him to "take her there," Dara helps Ben quickly spot a flaw in his approach. Now she can help craft an alternate approach.

DARA: Is that a problem?

BEN: Yeah, I think I'll lose them if I don't start by
         acknowledging what's been happening.

DARA: So what might you say instead?

BEN: What if I just lead with the punchline? "We've got
         tremendous potential on this team, and the ways
         we're communicating with each other—and failing
         to communicate—are getting in the way. We're all
         aware of it, and today I want to acknowledge it and
         get everyone's help in addressing and fixing it." Wow.
         That felt good. And scary.

BRAINSTORM WAYS TO MITIGATE RISKS

Once Ben identifies a better first step (leading with the punchline), Dara asks him to play it out—to rehearse likely scenarios.

DARA: So let's play this out. What do you think will happen
         after you kick off the meeting that way? What might
         Ramona do or say?

BEN: Hmm. She might take it as a personal attack. Like
         everyone knows that she's the squeaky wheel, and
         talking about the team's communication problem is
         just a coded way of criticizing her.

DARA: Given that you want Ramona to be part of the solu-
         tion, what might you do to get her to help instead of
         retreating into defensiveness?

BEN: I think I'd better talk with her first.

DARA: What do you want that conversation to accomplish?

BEN: I want her to see herself as a leader and take respon-
         sibility for changing her tone to be a more effective
         leader. I also want her to know that I appreciate her
         intentions, even though we've had a rough relationship.

The questioning that follows refines the plan to accomplish those goals.

DARA: What part of that do you think she needs to hear first?

BEN: I don't think she'll take kindly to me asking her to be more of a leader and to change her tone until I've—well, I'll say it—acknowledged how I've treated her.

DARA: What might that sound like? How would you start the conversation?

BEN: Well, it won't be a straight up apology. I don't want to give up my power to her, and that's how she'll read it.

DARA: What's the truth that you'd like her to know?

BEN: Basically, that a lot of what she's been trying to do for the team is stuff that we need, and I recognize that I've reacted poorly to it. And I'd like her to have more impact on the team, rather than less.

ROLE-PLAY TO IDENTIFY AND MITIGATE RISKS

When an option involves your partner having a conversation with someone, role-playing is almost always useful to identify and mitigate potential risks.

DARA: Shall we role-play your apology with Ramona? Why don't I be you, and you respond like you think Ramona would?

BEN: OK.

DARA: [as Ben] "Ramona, thanks for agreeing to meet with me. I've been thinking about how we've been interacting for these past months, and I realize that in many instances, I've tried to shut you down or marginalize your concerns. And I want to apologize for that."

BEN: [*as Ramona*] "Yeah, you have. I've felt isolated, and I know how you all talk about me when I'm not in the room."

DARA: Hmm. What might you say in response to that?

BEN: I'm not sure. Probably just repeat the apology. I mean, I can't expect her to forgive me and move on in a hot second.

DARA: [*as Ben*] "You're right. We've been more focused on keeping the peace among ourselves than facing some tough realities."

BEN: [*as Ramona*] "So what do you want? Should I forgive you, and then things go back to the way they were?"

DARA: [*as Ben*] "That's not what I want. But I also want you to know that it's a two-way street. I've felt frustrated at the way you communicate with us, even though I know you're making good points."

You'll often get pushback when you offer to role-play conversations because it's an uncomfortable thing to do. Because people don't want to look foolish, they will often decline the request.

DARA: Shall we role-play your apology with Ramona? Why don't I be you, and you respond like you think Ramona would?

BEN: Nah, that's OK. I got this.

Let me be blunt: They don't got this.

When the next step is a challenging conversation, it's almost always extremely eye-opening to do a dry run via a role-play. I might point out that if they're unwilling to have a pretend conversation with me, it's unlikely they'll get up the courage to have the real conversation.

Sometimes, rather than argue this point, I advocate for the role-play by observing that it will be useful to rehearse the conversation so they'll have a realistic and accurate sense of what they're choosing. Don't insist, but encourage them to give it a try.

WHEN THEY DON'T KNOW WHAT TO DO

Even after coming up with several promising options, sometimes people will say that they don't know what to do.

When someone tells me they don't know what to do, I ask a simple question that works almost 100 percent of the time: "If you did know, what would it be?" And then I wait.

I know; it's a little strange. It shouldn't work, but it does.

Here's why it does: It lowers the bar for your partner. They don't have to commit to the "right" answer; instead, they're answering a low-risk hypothetical.

Another way to break a decision deadlock is to suggest they flip a coin. Heads, choose Option A; tails, choose Option B.

When the coin lands, they'll have a reaction to the outcome. Ask them about it. Often, they will know what they really want to do when an outside source dictates their actions to them.

Let's say the coin lands on tails, indicating that Ben should hire a coach for Ramona. He looks down at the eagle and shakes his head.

BEN: I don't think that's a great idea.
DARA: What about that won't work?

The question "What about that won't work?" points your partner to certain risks and problems. Often, that's enough to help them select an option that mitigates those risks and avoids those problems.

WHEN YOU THINK THEY'RE MAKING A MISTAKE

Sometimes you'll disagree with your partner's choice. You may feel the urge to offer advice or to criticize their thinking. Don't. The truth is, you're not a fortune-teller; you don't know for certain what will work and what won't.

If you have concerns that your partner doesn't consider spontaneously, raise them. If you have experience and perspective that can help them make a more informed choice, share them.

But do so in the form of honest statements and questions, not sneaky ways of making or proving a point. In the dialogue, Ben quickly realizes that his planned opening ("Today I want us to mold ourselves into a high-performing team") is not a great idea. Without any prompting from Dara, he pivots to a different opening, one that he's much more comfortable with. And Dara reinforces his choice by pointing out that it has the added benefit of stretching him in a direction he already identified he wants to go: telling his truth even when doing so will cause discomfort.

Don't:

BEN: I think the team meeting where we air everything is probably the key step.

DARA: Oh, no, don't do that. Ramona will be blindsided and will naturally assume that this is a thinly veiled attack on her.

Do:

BEN: I think the team meeting where we air everything is probably the key step.

DARA: Take me there. How do you kick things off? Let's play it out.

As Ben describes the scene in detail, he becomes aware of some of the risks on his own. Again, you don't need to agree or disagree with your partner's assessment. Keep asking questions to make sure that they think through all the possible risks and rewards of their choice.

Don't:

DARA: So let's play this out. What do you think will happen after you kick off the meeting that way? What might Ramona do or say?

BEN: She'll probably sit with her arms folded, scowling, just like always.

DARA: Well, I wouldn't blame her. She'll probably be thinking that you've called this whole meeting just to attack her lack of team spirit.

Do:

DARA: So let's play this out. What do you think will happen after you kick off the meeting that way? What might Ramona do or say?

BEN: She'll probably sit with her arms folded, scowling, just like always.

DARA: Is there a risk that she'll feel blindsided? And assume that since the rest of the team really gets along, this is just an attack on her?

BEN: Yeah, I suppose. I guess the team meeting is a bad idea.

DARA: I don't know whether it's a bad idea or a good idea. But how might you mitigate the risk of Ramona feeling blindsided and refusing to participate?

BEN: I could start by owning some of the ways I've contributed to the problem. I could take responsibility proactively.

DARA: Great. Anything else?

BEN: Well, now that I think about it, I should probably have a private conversation with Ramona before the team meeting so she won't feel like it's an attack. That way, she won't need to act so defensively.

Dara truly doesn't know the best path forward, and she's not passing judgment on Ben's opinions. Instead, she's being open and honest about her concerns and raising them as hypotheses to be considered and perhaps tested.

Remember to keep the ball in their court. You are helping them choose, not choosing for them and not trying to convince them to choose one option over another. If they sense that you have an agenda, they'll respond with resistance or loss of ownership. The former puts you at odds, and the latter drastically decreases the probability that they will follow through on the plan.

You maintain your ability to help by expressing humility here. Even if you *know* the right option, even if you can clearly see the visionary brilliance of the move you want your partner to make, don't get seduced into pushing it. That would put you squarely in critic mode, not something you want, especially given all the work you've already done to be their ally.

CHAPTER 26

TASK 3: COMMIT TO THE PLAN

WHAT, HOW, AND WHEN?

Once your partner has chosen a plan of action, you're almost done. There's just one last bit: get them to commit to a specific, observable action by a deadline.

The two keys to this part of the process are commitment and accountability. By asking for specific actions on a specific timeline, you are asking them to make a commitment. But be careful not to do it in such a way that puts you in the role of hall monitor. They're not accountable to *you*. They're accountable to *themselves*.

Even if the person you're helping is your child, don't get drawn into acting like "the parent" at this point. You are not going to reward them for honoring their commitment or punish them for failing to do so. Do not shame them, nag them, or remind them about what they've committed to do. And don't express any doubt about whether they're going to do it.

Let's see how Dara gets Ben to commit without making him accountable *to her*.

DARA: Great. So let's nail this down: what exactly are you going to do, and when?

BEN: As soon as we finish here, I'll call Ramona and ask her to meet with me on Monday afternoon. In that meeting, I'll say what we talked about: that a lot of what she's been trying to do for the team is stuff that we need, and I recognize that I've reacted poorly to it, and I'd like her to have more impact on the team, not less. And then, if she's willing, I'll ask her to help me design a team meeting to kick off the process of reconciliation and moving forward.

DARA: Great. On a scale of 1 to 10, with 1 being not at all confident and 10 being 100 percent confident, how confident are you that you will do this?

BEN: I'd say an 8.

DARA: OK. Why isn't it a 10?

BEN: Well, Ramona might say she's too busy to meet, and can I just send an email or message her on Slack.

DARA: What could you do then?

BEN: I guess I could write down what I was going to tell her.

DARA: Would that have the impact you're hoping for?

BEN: No, definitely not.

DARA: So what do you want to do?

BEN: I'll be firm on the call—I'd like to talk to her about how the team is doing, and I want her input. I think she can hear that without getting defensive.

DARA: So how confident are you now?

BEN: 9 out of 10.

DARA: 9? Why not 10? What's getting in the way of your total confidence?

BEN: As much as I want to do this, I can see myself chickening out when I have to sit down with Ramona.

DARA: OK, take me there. You've invited her to talk. She sits down. You're about to speak. What's the first thing you want to say? The exact words.

BEN: "Ramona, I've come to realize that . . ." Oh, gosh, I've forgotten the words.

DARA: That's OK. Why don't you take a moment and think. Then write down what you want to say, and try it out on me.

BEN: [*Thinking, then writing, then reading*] "Ramona, I know I haven't always acted like it, but I want you to have a greater impact on the team. I've reacted poorly to some of the ways you've been trying to make us successful, and I'd like to talk with you about ways that you and I can work together better."

DARA: Now that you've got it down on paper, how confident are you that you can say that to her?

BEN: 10 out of 10. I'm actually kind of excited to do this.

DARA: And how confident are you about having the whole conversation once you've started?

BEN: 10 out of 10. I think that the scary part is just getting the first sentence out.

DARA: Great. One more question: How are you going to evaluate your results? Remember, this is all an experiment, so you're going to want some way to collect the data to see how it worked.

BEN: Well, one thing is if Ramona agrees to work with me on this. Another is whether the team is on board.

DARA: The way you describe your team, they'll probably say yes even if they mean no. Is that fair?

BEN: [*Chuckling*] Yeah, you're probably right. I'll have to see some real change in their behavior before I believe they're truly on board.

DARA: How could you assess that?

BEN: Well, by looking.

DARA: What types of behaviors specifically would you be looking for?

BEN: Disagreeing with each other. Not accepting the first suggestion. Proactively sharing their concerns. And being OK with being disagreed with.

DARA: Can you set up a process where people can give and receive feedback on how they're doing and how they might continue to improve?

BEN: I can model that and ask for feedback about how I'm doing with being more forthright in my communications. And invite them to pick one thing they can do better and get feedback from the rest of us. If Ramona's in, she can work on disagreeing more respectfully.

DARA: That sounds great. It's not you changing her, but everyone working on getting better together.

BEN: Yeah, we can even have a part of the weekly meeting where people share examples of us communicating more openly and respectfully. I can see how approaching it as a team can make it part of our culture going forward.

DARA: That's awesome. I'm really excited for you! Hey, would you call me on Tuesday afternoon or Wednesday to let me know how it goes? If you don't want to, that's totally fine—this is about you, not me. But if it would be helpful, or if you just want to talk about how it went, I'd love to hear how it goes.

BEN: Sure thing. I'll reach out on Wednesday, after I've had some time to unwind and reflect on the meeting. Hey, I really appreciate this!

DARA: My pleasure!

Dara helped Ben accomplish a lot in their short exchange. He identified exactly what he was going to do and improved his plan by identifying and mitigating risks. Through role-playing, he got an even clearer picture of how he would approach things, feeling a high level of confidence about the revised plan, with a system to measure and assess the results.

To help your partner conclude with that same level of commitment and confidence, begin with a straightforward question. Ask them what they're going to do, and when.

DARA: Great. So let's nail this down: What exactly are you
        going to do, and when?

If their answer isn't specific in terms of what, how, and when, then ask clarifying questions. Don't let them slide by with a vague intention and no deadline. It will be impossible for them to accurately gauge how likely they are to follow through on something when they aren't clear on what exactly, and when exactly, so their assessment of their confidence level will be meaningless.

Don't:

BEN: I'll have that conversation with Ramona next week.
DARA: Great! How confident are you that you'll do it?

Do:

BEN: I'll have that conversation with Ramona next week.
DARA: What's the first step?
BEN: I'll call her and let her know that I want to
        meet with her.
DARA: When will you do that?
BEN: Today.
DARA: Great, when today?
BEN: By the end of the day.
DARA: And what about the meeting itself? How will you
        start it off?
BEN: I'll tell her that a lot of what she's been trying to do
        for the team is stuff that we need, and I recognize that

I've reacted poorly to it, and I'd like her to have more impact on the team, not less. And then, if she's willing, I'll ask her to help me design a team meeting to kick off the process of reconciliation and moving forward.

THE POWER OF WHEN/THEN

Committing to the plan can be straightforward when the plan your partner commits to involves a specific event or action that they initiate: having a conversation, writing an email, buying a pair of running shoes.

Ben has committed to two actions: talking with Ramona and raising the communication issue with his team. In both cases, he's clear exactly what's going to trigger his action. When he returns to his office after talking with Dara, Ben will call Ramona. When the team next meets, he will share his observations and requests.

But that's just the beginning of the change, not the end. For Ben to become a more effective leader, he's going to need to change his behavior on an ongoing basis in ways that will, at times, be unfamiliar and uncomfortable. He'll have to become more assertive. He will have to disagree and risk offending teammates. And he will have to give feedback to Ramona in a way that preserves and enhances their relationship.

That's all new and challenging behavior for Ben—all the more so because those actions will need to be triggered by external events that aren't in his control. He can't add an event called "Disagree with Henry at 11:17 a.m. on Thursday" to his calendar. Instead, he has to be aware of the conditions or events that will trigger his new behavior. And that's awfully hard to do in the moment if he doesn't have a very specific plan for doing so.

An effective way to plan for and commit to these "triggered" behaviors is to create what NYU researcher Peter Gollwitzer calls "Implementation Intentions," more colloquially known as *When/Then* plans. Basically, the commitment goes like this:

When _____ [Trigger], *then I will* _____ [Specific Action].

The following are examples of When/Then plans:

"*When* I sense that the team is not addressing a risk, *then I will* speak up."

"*When* I feel the urge to interrupt a colleague, *then I will* take three deep breaths and jot down what I want to say in response, waiting until they're done before asking if I can share my own thoughts."

"*When* the waiter brings the dessert menu, *then I will* decline to take it and proactively order a cup of tea or black coffee."

GETTING TO LEVEL 10—OR AS CLOSE AS POSSIBLE

Once your partner has made a specific, observable, or measurable commitment with a specific date and time, ask how confident they are that they will follow through, on a scale from 1 to 10, with 1 being not at all and 10 being completely confident.

DARA: Great. On a scale of 1 to 10, with 1 being not at all confident and 10 being 100 percent confident, how confident are you that you will do this?

If their answer is a 10, great. Sometimes they'll even say 11.

One purpose of asking about their confidence is to maximize the odds that they'll actually do what they say they will. When someone declares out loud that they have no doubt that they will honor their commitment, it harnesses their sense of self-worth. People go to great lengths to act in ways consistent with their self-image. We do things—often challenging things—when we believe that we are the "kind of person" who does those things.

Another purpose is to surface any risks you may have missed and create a plan to mitigate them. If it's anything other than "10," ask why it isn't a 10. What's missing? What might get in the way? And what would close the gap to make it a 10?

Then work with them, in the same way you did when they were choosing from among options, to address those obstacles.

If the obstacles are procedural (not sure how to do it, don't know how the other person will respond, don't know if all resources will be in place in time), then you can return to the strategies you used when making your choice. Refine the option to deal with those issues. Identify a lower rung on the ladder. Identify a necessary "pre-step" that they have to accomplish prior to the action they want to commit to. Add other options.

If the obstacles involve fear of feeling something, then use the conversation to invite them to feel that feeling at a level of intensity they can handle as a form of "inoculation."

We saw an example of this in the stage of choosing, when Dara invited Ben to notice his physical sensations and pointed out that, in order to act courageously, he had to be willing to tolerate those sensations. Just the experience of not trying to avoid those sensations can free people to do things they never thought they could.

What if Ben couldn't get higher than 9, no matter how cleverly he and Dara tried to solve the issues that are keeping him in doubt? It's not always possible to get your partner to Level 10.

A personal example: I may commit to giving up sugar, but I know myself: Sometimes my resolve weakens in the moment when I'm tired and stressed and there's a really tempting dessert in front of me that other people are enjoying.

When you can't get your partner to a 10, don't despair. The very fact that they identify and acknowledge a risk means they're in a better position to manage it. Because Ben realizes that he might back out when the time comes to talk to Ramona, he can expect those feelings to arise and be prepared to ride them out.

He might take a selfie of himself with Dara for his phone's lock screen to remind him of the commitment he made in her presence. He might role-play the conversation a few more times with friends and family members to increase his comfort level.

And knowing he's scared can actually help Ben initiate the conversation with humility and kindness, qualities that might help Ramona open up rather than shut down in defensiveness.

HOW WILL THEY MEASURE SUCCESS?

Dara reminds Ben that what he's committing to is an experiment: a set of actions to test the hypothesis that he brainstormed when identifying options and making a choice. The hypothesis is, essentially: "This plan will help me get to my energizing outcome."

DARA: Great. You have a clear plan. One more question: how are you going to know if it worked? Remember, this is all an experiment.

BEN: Well, one thing is if Ramona agrees to work with me on this. Another is whether the team is on board.

DARA: The way you describe your team, they'll probably say yes even if they mean no. Is that fair?

BEN: [*Chuckling*] Yeah, you're probably right. I'll have to see some real change in their behavior before I believe they're truly on board.

DARA: What types of behaviors specifically would you be looking for?

BEN: Disagreeing with each other respectfully. Not accepting the first suggestion. Proactively sharing their concerns. Being forthright in their communications. And being OK with being disagreed with.

DARA: Can you set up a process where people can give and receive feedback on how they're doing on those specific behaviors? And how they might continue to improve?

BEN: I can model that and ask for feedback about how I'm doing on those behaviors. And invite them to get feedback from the rest of us. If Ramona's in, she can work on those same behaviors, especially disagreeing more respectfully.

DARA: That sounds great. It's not you changing her, but everyone working on getting better together.

BEN: Yeah, we can even have a part of the weekly meeting where people share examples of us demonstrating those specific behaviors. I can see how approaching it as a team can make it part of our culture going forward.

Helping your partner identify what they're going to measure, and how, will keep them focused on the outcome, enable them to gauge success, and course-correct as necessary.

AGREE TO FOLLOW UP

After your partner gets to a 10, or as close as you can help them get, your final goal is to offer to set up a follow-up conversation.

DARA: Great. I'm excited for you. Hey, would you call
        me on Tuesday afternoon or Wednesday to let me
        know how it goes? If you don't want to, that's totally
        fine—this is about you, not me. But if it would be
        helpful, or if you just want to talk about how it
        went, I'd love to hear how it goes.
BEN: Sure thing. Hey, I really appreciate this!

This follow-up does four important things.

First, even though your conversation partner is accountable
to themselves, not you, committing to tell you about their
outcome reinforces their commitment to themselves.

Second, it gives you a way to stay in the conversation so
you can continue to help them.

Third, it reinforces your allyship. It shows that you care.

Fourth, it makes explicit that you're not asking them to
"report" to you. You're not offering to be their conscience,
or their drill sergeant, or their parent (even if you are their
parent, don't get stuck in that role here). Instead, you're communicating that you're their ally. You care about them, and
their success, and you're invested at this point. Your willingness to stay involved comes from a place of caring, not obli-
gation. You're excited to hear how things progress, regardless
of outcome.

The key here is to provide the kind of support—not
supervision—that reinforces their accountability to themselves.

THE FOLLOW-UP

When they do follow up, listen to their account of what happened. Be curious, supportive, empathic, and nonjudgmental.

If the result was suboptimal, or a new wrinkle showed up,
or they're struggling to maintain progress, or it worked fab-
ulously and now they are facing a new challenge or problem or opportunity, go back to the beginning. Empathize, be

curious and nonjudgmental, and then ask: "Would you like help thinking this through?"

Follow-up conversations often move quickly and easily as you and your partner get to know the Four Steps. Your partner will anticipate your question about their energizing outcome. They will understand what you're asking when you talk about finding the opportunity in the problem. And they will offer a clear and detailed commitment to act after choosing an option from the ones they identify. I find that conversations with long-standing clients can take as little as a few minutes as we both know what to expect as we go through the Four Steps.

So, you may be wondering, how did Ben's eventual conversation with Ramona go? Ben followed up with a call to Dara on Tuesday afternoon, not 10 minutes after his conversation with Ramona. He was thrilled to share that after a rocky start, he helped Ramona identify an energizing outcome for herself: to become a stronger leader.

The problem, as she saw it, was an inexperienced team, which is why she was responding in frustration. Ben helped her turn that problem into an opportunity: What better way for Ramona to develop her leadership than to turn this group of inexperienced people into a high-performing team?

They developed her plan to do just that and ended the conversation connected to each other and excited to move forward. Visit BregmanPartners.com/change to see their full dialogue.

CHAPTER 27

TAKING THE FOUR STEPS INTO YOUR WORLD

YOU CAN CHANGE OTHER PEOPLE

Picking up this book was a significant act of caring, connection, and commitment to the people in your life. You decided to spend time and money to help them up their game. And you're now equipped to take the Four Steps into your world. On this practical journey, you've learned how to approach as an ally, focus on a positive outcome, find hidden opportunities, and guide the people you care about to life-changing action.

Don't worry about doing it perfectly. (There is no such thing.) Instead, just go out and do it. The way you'll master the process is by taking the risk to use it as a novice. Especially the first few times, it will be useful to draw on your own emotional courage as you apply the principles and steps. You don't have to memorize anything. You can be totally transparent about what you're doing—following a process you learned from this book. Feel free to use the book during your conversations. You can also print out a summary PDF worksheet at BregmanPartners.com/change.

Each situation will be a little different. You now have a clear picture of how Dara used the Four Steps to help Ben with his Ramona problem. And I've included snippets of dialogue from other conversations to illustrate the principles as well as the dos and the don'ts.

To show you how to apply the Four Steps in a wide variety of situations, I've shared nine complete Four Step dialogues—including detailed annotations—at BregmanPartners.com/change. Visit that page to eavesdrop on the following conversations:

- Ben's meeting with Ramona, in which he enlists her help in achieving a high-performing team
- A leader helping his employee take ownership of a project while sticking to his guns on a promised deliverable
- A sales manager refusing to do her employee's work for him and helping him develop independent capability as a salesperson
- A mentor guiding a CEO to use a frustrating workplace dynamic to future-proof her entire organization
- A spouse changing the tone of her marriage from anger and resentment to love and trust
- A friend helping a technologist transform his boss's boss from obstacle to advancement into patron of his career
- A Chief Marketing Officer helping his company's founding CEO, a bundle of agitated impatience, become more deliberate in finding a viable market
- An employee shifting a work-evading, excuse-making coworker into a valuable team player
- A sister repairing decades of damage in a conversation with her brother

I wrote this book to give you what the Four Steps have given me: opportunities to be of service, the thrill of seeing people achieve things that astound them, and the gratitude of brave souls who are sharing their unique gifts with the world.

You have in your hands the power to make a difference. Given how goodness and kindness and generosity have a way of rippling out in unknowable ways, it's impossible to know how big a difference. But one thing's for sure: In changing *your* world, you're changing *the* world.

I look forward to hearing how you use the Four Steps.

ACKNOWLEDGMENTS

HOWIE: I'm so ready to be done with this book. I really don't have energy for this part.

PETER: You sound exhausted. [*Empathy*] I know you can do it. [*Confidence*] Would you like help thinking this through? [*Permission*]

HOWIE: I see what you did there.

PETER: Seriously, we got a lot of help on this book.

HOWIE: We sure did. Starting with our long-suffering families.

PETER: That's easy. I'll start with my wife, Eleanor, who in the midst of her intensive anti-racism work, all-consuming training of our first-ever puppy, and focus on the kids, still managed to protect my last-minute writing marathon while finding time to give us notes on the book. And, of course, Daniel for being such a great example *in* the book. Sophia and Isabelle, I still write to impress you. Mama, it all started with you.

HOWIE: Mia, my wife, supported my writing for several months by bringing me daily green smoothies and rainbow bowls, and reminding me to get dressed for Zoom calls. She made literary lockdown not only bearable, but fun. I also want to thank my adult children, Yael and Elan, for moving out. Your bedrooms make a great office and home gym.

PETER: And to the readers who gave us invaluable advice and guidance on scandalously short notice.

HOWIE: My sister, Monica Jacobson, may have pulled a couple of all-nighters to go through the entire manuscript. She caught a bunch of errors and asked important questions whose answers made the work much clearer.

PETER: Pam Barkley, thank you for helping me see why this book means so much to me. Y'all should thank her too: she single-handedly shortened the manuscript by at least 20 percent, begging us to reduce repetitions. And to cut places where we repeated ourselves.

HOWIE: Danny Warshay, in addition to being a valuable resource on all things entrepreneurial and a stickler for clarity, also pursued a doggedly dogged crusade against glaringly unnecessary adverbs.

PETER: Many friends donated time out of their busy lives to help us improve the book: David Gallimore, Melinda Wolfe, Frank Wagner, Glenn Murphy, Jessica Gelson, Richard Osibanjo, Fernando Carillo, and Randall Tucker.

HOWIE: Glenn Livingston and Whitney Asnip helped us craft the marketing blurb that may have convinced you to get the book.

PETER: A huge thank you to my clients: the early ones who partnered with me (and sometimes suffered through) figuring out what worked, and my current ones with whom I am still learning. A particular thank you to Brian Gaffney, Don Kania, Marc Boroditsky, David Nevins, Cam Weber, Chris Spade, Juan Martin, and so many others, for your commitment to being exceptional leaders and stellar human beings.

HOWIE: Here's to my coach training students, whose questions and objections keep forcing me to explain better. And to my clients for their courage, commitment, and vulnerability. A particular nod to Ian Lawton, whom we called Ian in the book to protect his privacy, for allowing me to use a snippet of one of our conversations to illustrate a point.

PETER: Thank you, those of you who have come to the Bregman Leadership Intensive and the Bregman Leadership Coach Training. Your courage in learning, growing, and changing in both professional and deeply personal ways inspires me and this book. You are proof that yes, you *can* change other people—and the world.

HOWIE: Working with Jim Levine, our agent, was a total blast.

PETER: He's the best, isn't he? Jim really guided the vision of this book from the very beginning, through countless email exchanges and Zoom meetings. It's scary to think of all the dead ends he helped us avoid.

HOWIE: And we loved working with the team at Wiley. Richard Narramore, our editor, changed everything when he gave us the phrase critic to ally, among many invaluable contributions. What a joy to partner with you! Victoria Anllo and Deborah Schindler took such exquisite care of the manuscript as they shepherded it to publication. And Angela Morrison copyedited (is that one word or two, Angela?) the manuscript to as close to grammatical and stylistic perfection as our casual voices would allow.

PETER: These acknowledgments are going to double the length of our book! But perhaps most important, I do want to thank some of my mentors as this book is a culmination of a lifetime of learning. Marshall Goldsmith, in addition to penning the Foreword, you more or less created the field of executive coaching. I continue to learn from you in every one of our conversations. Ann Bradney, you continue to touch my life, push my thinking, and raise the bar for how I show up. Beth Fletcher and Andy Geller, you got me started on the right foot and I continue to feel your impact in all my work.

HOWIE: I've got to give a shout-out to Josh LaJaunie, whose journey from morbid obesity to the cover of *Runner's World* has inspired thousands—including me—to rethink our own potential for change. And, gosh, Peter, you've had a huge positive impact on my life for over two decades. Working on this book has been an honor and an education: not just in your brilliant methodology, but your willingness to keep questioning and challenging yourself to get better. Your commitment to feedback, growth, and courage are contagious, and I'm honored to be your co-conspirator, coauthor, and friend. [*Punches Peter in the arm to cover his embarrassment*]

PETER: I'm glad I get the last word here! I am filled with joy when I think about the years of our friendship and collaboration. What a gift. You are a terrific partner, not just because of how smart you are and how hard you work, but most important because of how committed you are to being a force of good in the world. You care. And that is the soul of everything we do together. It's what makes it worthwhile. And your sense of humor makes it fun. I too am honored—and grateful—to be your co-conspirator, coauthor, and friend.

ABOUT THE AUTHORS

PETER BREGMAN

Peter Bregman is the CEO of Bregman Partners. He coaches, writes, teaches, and speaks, mostly about leadership and also about life. His sweet spot is as a strategic thought partner to successful people who care about being exceptional leaders and stellar human beings.

Peter is recognized as the #1 executive coach in the world by Leading Global Coaches. He coaches C-level executives in many of the world's premier organizations, including Citi, CBS, Mars, Showtime, AMC Networks, Allianz, Electronic Arts, Pearson, and Twilio, to name a few. He is also a ski coach on the weekends in the winter (but definitely *not* the #1 ski coach in the world).

Peter is the best-selling author of five books including *Leading with Emotional Courage* and *18 Minutes*. His work appears frequently in *Harvard Business Review, BusinessWeek, Fast Company, Psychology Today,* and *Forbes*. He has also been featured on CNN and NPR.

Peter created and leads the #1 leadership development program in the world, the Bregman Leadership Intensive, and trains leaders and managers on the Four Steps through the Bregman Leadership Coach Training program.

Peter is the host of the Bregman Leadership Podcast, with over 1.5 million downloads. He has given four TEDx talks and regularly delivers keynotes for associations like SHRM and companies, including Coca-Cola, the Discovery Network, L'Oréal, Deloitte, and Fidelity, among others.

Peter earned his M.B.A. from Columbia University and his B.A. from Princeton University.

Peter lives in New York City with his wife, three kids, and new puppy, Maeve (his first dog ever). He reads, runs, skis, bikes, hikes, and tries to follow his own advice.

He can be reached at www.bregmanpartners.com.

HOWIE JACOBSON

Howie Jacobson, PhD, is an executive coach to clients ranging from startup founders to established and rising Fortune 100 leaders. He is director of coaching at Bregman Partners and head coach at the Healthy Minds Initiative.

Howie is the author of *AdWords For Dummies*; coauthor of *Sick to Fit* and *Use the Weight to Lose the Weight*, with Josh LaJaunie; contributing author to *Whole: Rethinking the Science of Nutrition* and *The Low Carb Fraud*, both by T. Colin Campbell, Ph.D.; and *Proteinaholic* by Garth Davis, M.D. Howie's writings have also appeared in *Fast Company* and *Harvard Business Review*.

He hosts the Plant Yourself Podcast, where he interviews remarkable people engaged in healing at the individual, institutional, and planetary level.

Howie earned his M.P.H. and Ph.D. in Health Studies from Temple University and his B.A. from Princeton University.

He lives in rural North Carolina with his wife, where he writes, gardens, plays Ultimate Frisbee, runs, fiddles, and loads the dishwasher correctly.

His mission includes helping kind and generous people grow their capability and scale their influence, sharing the joys of a healthy life, and reintroducing people to their most authentic, best selves. He can be reached at www. askHowie.com.